JAMES NELSON BARKER

JAMES NELSON BARKER

1784-1858

WITH A REPRINT OF HIS COMEDY

TEARS AND SMILES

BY PAUL H. MUSSER
ASSISTANT PROFESSOR OF ENGLISH
UNIVERSITY OF PENNSYLVANIA

PHILADELPHIA
UNIVERSITY OF PENNSYLVANIA PRESS
LONDON: HUMPHREY MILFORD, OXFORD UNIVERSITY PRESS

1929

Copyright, 1929
UNIVERSITY OF PENNSYLVANIA PRESS
Printed in the United States of America by
Lancaster Press, Inc., Lancaster, Pa.

30-4244

PS
1065
B83
Z7

CONTENTS

54675

I

INTRODUCTION

James Nelson Barker's contributions to the American drama are the most permanent of the results of his numerous activities. In the first quarter of the nineteenth century Barker and John Howard Payne were the leaders of the two contrasting influences that motivated American playwrights. Barker is the foremost of those whose drama primarily drew upon native interest and tradition, while Payne represents the group of dramatists that depended largely upon foreign inspiration for their plays. Because of the national tendency of the period to look to Europe for standards of taste, and because of a provincial feeling of inferiority that led to a general deprecation of anything American in literature and art, Barker's writing assumes something of the nature of a literary war for independence. He deplored our tendency to become "mental colonists." It was for the very reason that he himself was widely read that he was keenly aware of the benumbing effects of slavish imitation in national literature. In his own writing he did all in his power to remedy affairs and in energetically appealing to Americans generally gave expression to the same ideas on the subject of literary independence that Lowell and Emerson later advocated. This Americanism of Barker's was not provincial in its insistence upon exclusive use of native themes. He himself uses English subject matter in one instance and Spanish in another. It simply stood for a more reasonable, justly proportioned use of American material by American authors in the development of a national literature in keeping with the social, economic and political principles developed in the United States. It stimulated him to write the best play composed in America before 1825.

This patriotic independence in letters was an inevitable outgrowth of Barker's training. He was brought up a social and political democrat and drilled in the principles of the American Revolution. His love for independence carried him into the war of 1812. It led to active support of the Greek cause in 1824, the French Revolution of 1848 and a sympathy with independence and freedom wherever found. His belief in democracy is a constant, even persistent note in his occasional verse, biographical prose, orations, political articles and criticism. It certainly is the actuating principle behind the incidents of his personal and public career. It explains his lifelong altruism and belligerent partisanship.

The affairs of public office and political leadership absorbed the larger proportion of Barker's time and energy. The necessities of political organization through meetings, committees and correspondence made large inroads upon his attention. The duties of an alderman, the administration of the mayoralty during a turbulent period in Philadelphia's history demanded much of both time and energy. The combined requirements of the office of Collector of the Port of Philadelphia and local representation of the national administration in Jackson's day were heavy and consuming. The routine work of the position of First Comptroller of the U. S. Treasury and his duties in the office of the Secretary of the Treasury during the closing years of his life left Barker with little freedom for other pursuits.

The composition of some ten plays, the adaptation or Americanization of others; the writing of prologues for fellow dramatists, and the authorship of an extended series of articles of dramatic criticism, are his main contributions to dramatic literature; which, however, was only one of Barker's literary interests. He wrote history, biography, patriotic songs, other lyric, occasional and satirical verse; controversial articles, orations, and miscellaneous prose. The leisure for the making of these must have been so limited as to render their high quality not less than remarkable.

In public affairs, private life, literary production and general traits James Nelson Barker is a thorough product of the finest forces of the so called "Middle American Period" that historians and biographers have recently exploited as so significant in the building of American culture. His versatile, energetic personality had points of contact with nearly all the facets of his age. Political, literary, altruistic and friendly concerns brought him in personal touch with all the prominent men of the era. His career thoroughly exemplifies the times and the nation.

Yet in spite of his importance the existing material upon the life of Barker was found to be surprisingly meagre and inaccurate. The most extended biographical account was limited to a few pages in Henry Simpson's *Lives of Eminent Philadelphians now Deceased.* Little was known of his later career in Washington and what had been written on the subject of it proved largely guess work. His verse and his biographical, critical, and political prose had been largely lost sight of. His dramatic work, however, has been thoroughly estimated in Professor A. H. Quinn's *A History of the American Drama from the Beginning to the Civil War.* His drama *Superstition* has been reprinted in Professor Quinn's *Representative American Plays,* his *The Indian Princess,* in M. J. Moses' *Representative Plays by American Dramatists.*

Tears and Smiles, here reproduced, was Barker's first staged play. It is the only one of his surviving dramas on an American theme not reprinted. It has a particular interest in relationship with its author's position as an advocate of the native play. It is not merely an example of the early American comedy of manners, but is the beginning of the conscious effort to carry on a crusade for American drama that, as has been pointed out, created one of the two great influences during the first quarter of that century. In view of this it seems particularly appropriate that the scene should be laid in Barker's native city and should make use of Philadelphia customs as its subject. It is his single dramatic treatment of that place. It has, further, expository importance as one of the early steps in the development of the so called Yankee plays and in the growth of social satire. In addition, despite obvious faults, it possesses an inherent interest that makes the depiction of contemporary manners and social standards and such parts as that of Widow Freegrace and Rangely worthy of serious attention. Barker's account of the origin of *Tears and Smiles* and of the opening performances has been included as the most suitable prelude to it. With the exception of a few corrections of quite evident typograpical errors, and a limited number of alterations in punctuation, for the sake of clarity, the text of the play conforms as accurately as possible to that of 1808, the only surviving form.

Assistance has been given most generously in the preparation of the whole work. I most gratefully acknowledge my indebtedness to Miss Josephine Keys of Baltimore, the granddaughter of the dramatist, whose kindness in the loan of manuscripts has been an indispensable aid. Her interest and care in the matters of family tradition, genealogy and helpful suggestions also have been invaluable. I sincerely appreciate, likewise, the help of Mrs. Dayton Ward of Washington, an old friend of the Barker family, who first gave me an introduction to Miss Keys and furnished much information concerning the family history. The co-operation of the staffs at the Library of the University of Pennsylvania, the Ridgway Library and the Historical Society of Pennsylvania has been helpful and productive. The permission of Mr. Lincoln Acker, Collector of the Port of Philadelphia, to search the archives of the Custom House resulted in the finding of many facts of Barker's official life.

I wish further to express my thanks to several members of the Department of English at the University of Pennsylvania who have given willingly of their valuable counsel. My gratitude to Professor Arthur H. Quinn arises from the most compelling of all my obligations. He not only suggested the subject of Barker, but guided the general development of the work, placed his complete knowledge of the American drama at my disposal, and freely gave of his experience. Professor Albert C. Baugh contributed several important suggestions particularly in reference to the bibliographical material. To Professor John C. Mendenhall, Assistant Professor Harold S. Stine, and Assistant Professor Edward S. Bradley, I am especially obligated for their most generous assistance in the reading of proof.

II

THE EARLY BACKGROUND OF PATRIOTISM AND POLITICS

THE inheritance and training of James Nelson Barker developed traits and a point of view that plainly account for his position as advocate of native material in the American drama. His success in treating the Indian, Colonial history, contemporary society and politics in plays, prose, and verse grows directly from his early environment of patriotism and politics. The time and place of his early years were intimately associated with the men and affairs that largely determined the character of the nation.

Philadelphia as the largest and wealthiest city of the country was a center of political, literary and social activity. It was the scene of the struggles of the new government for existence. During the decade when the city was the capital, national traditions were forming and the future leaders of the United States were emerging. Only naturally also did it become the literary capital, a position which it retained for nearly a generation after the seat of government was moved to Washington. In turn Philadelphia's social life assumed a prestige in keeping with the city's political and literary influence. The somewhat aristocratic nature of the town made, through resistance to certain more democratic elements, for sturdiness and growth among the democratic, less wealthy citizens. Prominent among these was a wit, popular orator and veteran of the Revolution, John Barker, the father of James Nelson Barker. He was a town character and Democratic politician with a large personal following and belligerent patriotic views.

Although John Barker was noted for his fiery anti-British

attitude he was a descendant of the Barkers and Wades, English colonists in Salem County, New Jersey. Samuel Wade had migrated from England in 1675 and his youngest granddaughter, Mary, married John Barker about 1736. The second son of this marriage, born about 1746, was this anti-English patriot—supposed to have had a birthright membership in the Society of Friends.[1] By 1765 he had moved to Philadelphia and had become sergeant in Captain Richard Peters' First Volunteer Corps of the city.[2] He married Mary Nelson in St. Michael's and Zion Lutheran Church of Philadelphia on July 13, 1769.[3] He was a tailor by trade and kept a shop until the beginning of the Revolution.

John Barker's interest in the militia was a sustained, active one. He was a private in the Pennsylvania Militia at the close of the year 1776[4] and had risen to be first lieutenant in the Fourth Battalion of the Philadelphia Associators by August of 1777.[5] When the British took Philadelphia, Mrs. Barker had been unable to leave and John Barker, disguised as a farmer, entered the city and joined her. On the first rainy day, with his wife at his side, he put a blanket over their heads and drove out of the city in a cart, being obliged to drive up along the Delaware as far as Trenton before daring to cross to comparative safety in the woods of New Jersey. He made several other excursions into Philadelphia for information until the British discovered this and placed a reward upon his head. He was at Valley Forge and in the Battle of Germantown.[6]

1 Biographical sketch—Philadelphia *North American and United States Gazette,* Jan. 14, 1876.

2 *Pennsylvania Magazine of History and Biography,* XLIX (1925), 91–92.

3 *Pennsylvania Archives,* 2d series, IX, 338.

4 *Ibid.,* 6th series, I, 474.

5 *Pennsylvania Magazine of History and Biography,* XLIX (1925), 91–92.

6 *North American and United States Gazette,* Philadelphia, Jan. 14, 1876.

By the time of the birth of his fourth son, James Nelson Barker, on June 17, 1784, he had been commissioned Captain of the Fourth Company, First Battalion of the Philadelphia Militia.[7] He had re-opened his tailor shop at the "Sign of St. Tammany" on Arch Street, a popular inn of which he was proprietor and which was a gathering place for the Democratic politicians.[8] During the yellow fever epidemic of 1793, he and his wife remained in the city, nursed patients in the hospitals and aided in the general charity work.[9] In the following year his loyalty was again proved by service in the Whiskey Rebellion and recognized by his election as Lieutenant-Colonel in the Pennsylvania Militia.[10] He was made high sheriff of Philadelphia on his return to the city that same year and held the office until 1797.[11] This position, with his vigorous, aggressive political principles had made him a force in the Democratic, then Republican, party by 1800. He was, however, defeated for the Pennsylvania Assembly that fall. Governor Thomas McKean appointed him a Philadelphia Alderman on October 22, 1800.[12] He had his office at his own house, 114 N. 9th Street, southwest corner of 9th and Race streets, whither he had removed after giving up the inn.

John Barker's ability as a stump speaker, his sarcastic wit and convivial exploits combined with his belligerent patriotism made him a town character of great popularity—a popularity that determined the trend of his whole career. "Political damnation to all political hypocrites" [13] was one of his political

7 *Pennsylvania Archives,* 6th series, III, 947.

8 White's *Philadelphia Directory* 1785, p. 8 and *Pennsylvania Magazine of History and Biography,* XXVI (1902), 223.

9 "A Short Account of the Yellow Fever in 1793," *Philadelphia Gazette,* April 17, 1830.

10 *Pennsylvania Archives,* 6th series, IV, 64.

11 Thompson Westcott, *Civil Officers of Philadelphia and Pennsylvania,* ms, II, 5.

12 *Aurora,* Philadelphia, October 14, November 1, 1800.

13 *Ibid.,* April 21, 1807.

slogans illustrative of his general tone and that of his supporters. It was his personal popularity, largely, that created him Brigadier-General of the First Brigade of the First Division of the Philadelphia Militia in 1802 [14] and gave him a second turbulent term as sheriff from 1803–1807.[15] His appointment, from among several candidates, as Major-General of the First Division of the Philadelphia Militia, June 5, 1807,[16] led to bitter attacks characteristic of the virulent personal press of the day. He was depicted as a " miserable major general, with a puerile vanity, that would disgrace a boarding school miss " [17] and said to be " no more qualified than an ape." He was supported, on the other hand, by the newly established *Democratic Press* and the physical might of his friends—one of them, Vogdes by name, having had a physical encounter with William Duane, editor of the *Aurora*, that was news material for several days.[18] John Barker was, as a matter of fact, both skillful and reliable as a military officer. These attacks and disputes were simply an expression of the bitter feeling generated by approaching elections.

As part of his contribution to these same elections John Barker composed *The Political Creed of an Old Revolutionary Officer* [19] in which his thirty-one articles of belief were packed with contentious material and stated with caustic directness. " I believe there has not been an election since we were a nation of more importance, and which called more for the united strength of republican candour than the approaching one, for toryism, traitorism, Englishism and federalism (so called), aided by lies, intrigue and gold, will be played off against honest Democracy " [20] was not the sort of statement partisan editors read

14 *Pennsylvania Archives,* 6th series, IV, 758.

15 Wescott, *op. cit.,* II, 5.

16 *Pennsylvania Magazine of History and Biography,* XLIX (1925), 91–92.

17 *Aurora,* July 17, 1807.

18 *Democratic Press,* Philadelphia, July 22, 30, and August 1, 1807.

19 *Ibid.,* July 28, 1808.

20 *Ibid.*

complacently. Such terms as traitor, miscreant, blasphemer, and apostate were generously applied in attack and defense.[21] Popular opinion, however, seemed to be with General Barker, as on October 18, 1808, the Select and Common councils elected him mayor of the city.[22] The excitement over the Embargo Bills led, in January, 1809, to a wild demonstration on their behalf that was led in Philadelphia by Mayor Barker followed by the customary frenzied outbursts from the opposition press.[23] His thoroughness and efficiency as an administrator of the city's affairs are indicated in his communications to the city councils and his serious concern over the welfare of his fellow citizens.[24] He was re-elected mayor October, 1809.[25] He served on nearly all of the party committees of the period and officiated at most of the public meetings held in the city. His concerns were, at times, with national questions. He was interested and active in the fight over the rechartering of the United States Bank in 1810; organized town meetings in protest against a renewal and addressed a public letter to his friend, James Madison.[26] This was an opposition that was supported by his son until the final smashing of the bank by Andrew Jackson.

When the War of 1812 began, John Barker was for the third time mayor of the city. With habitual promptness he busied himself in all the activities in support of the contest. As early as June 3, 1812, he aided in organizing a committee "for the preservation of domestic order and tranquility" during the absence of the younger citizens in the Army.[27] He was chairman of the "American Patriotic Fund Association of Philadelphia" to aid the families of soldiers and sailors. He took a

21 *Ibid.,* August 1 and 15, 1808.

22 *Ibid.,* October 18, 1808.

23 Scharf and Westcott, *History of Philadelphia,* I, 539.

24 See ms letters, Papers of the Mayors, Historical Society of Pennsylvania.

25 *Democratic Press,* October 17, 1809.

26 *Ibid.,* February 28, 1810.

27 *Ibid.,* June 3, 1812.

leading part in both the official and unofficial celebrations of victories. He proclaimed general illuminations of public and private buildings in honor of Perry's victory on Lake Erie,[28] Harrison's success in Michigan [29] and made use of other occasions as means of rallying patriotic sentiment. His personal enthusiasm now and then found outlet. When the news of the capture of the British frigate *La Guerrière* by the *Constitution* reached Philadelphia, he called at an inn he sometimes frequented to sink the Guerrière in toasts. The landlady knowing his habits admonished him—"Take care, General! take care, General! that in sinking the Guerrière you do not destroy the Constitution!" [30]

In the mayoralty election by city councils held in October, 1813, he failed of re-election [31] and returned to the office of alderman. His support of the war continued unabated after his retirement as executive. In 1814 he participated in town meetings for the purpose of organizing further defense of the city [32] and was a member of the famous committee of defense [33] that directed the entire war energies of the city. He was toasted frequently at this time—"the hero of the revolution, the humane sheriff and mayor" [34] being among the toasts given. His political interests continued through chairmanships of local committees and town meetings until his resignation as an alderman in the spring of 1817 when his son, James Nelson Barker, was appointed in his place.[35] The period of retirement was shortly brought to a close by his death on April 3, 1818. The city officials, the mili-

28 *Aurora,* September 24, 1813.

29 *Ibid.,* October 19, 1813.

30 Henry Simpson, *Lives of Eminent Philadelphians now Deceased,* pp. 25–26.

31 *Aurora,* October 20, 1813.

32 *General Committee of Defence,* ms minutes of proceedings, Historical Society of Pennsylvania.

33 *Democratic Press,* September 7, 1814.

34 *Aurora,* November 5, 1813.

35 *Democratic Press,* April 8, 1817.

tary organizations, the Masonic orders, and the benevolent societies of which he was a member paid homage to his memory. Among other newspaper comment the *Democratic Press* presented its opinion of General Barker in the following notice: "Died—This morning at 2 o'clock Maj. Gen. John Barker—72 yrs. He had been confined for some months with an asthmatic complaint, to which he fell a victim. The deceased was an officer in the Revolutionary Army; one whose bravery and devotion to the cause of his country were as unquestionable as the goodness and generosity of his heart were undisputable. Few men have ever lived who were naturally so gifted as a popular orator as was General Barker. Words, the choicest and most energetic, flowed copiously, almost spontaneously from his lips; they were those above all others best adapted to affect the heart and impress the memory, and were accompanied by an appropriateness of action and expression of countenance which always gave to them their greatest possible effect.

"General Barker had been Sheriff of the city and county of Philadelphia; more than once Mayor of the city and had received many other testimonials of confidence and esteem from his fellow citizens. He lived much beloved, and will yet live long in the feelings and recollections of those who knew his public services, his private worth and his many estimable qualities."

It was this man with his vivid personality, his contentious support of freedom, his patriotism, and democratic principles who trained James Nelson Barker in party loyalty and political beliefs, shaped his standards of honor and duty, gave him an ideal, and was closer to him than any other man. The versatile career of the son takes its set and tone from the unusually intimate association with the environment of these early days—the patriotism and politics, the altruism and honesty of John Barker.

III

LITERATURE AND DEMOCRATS

THE inheritance of James Nelson Barker by way of high personal honor and generosity, social democracy and patriotism is embodied in his literary and political points of view. He, further, possessed the fiery traits of his father's personality but added to these an ameliorating polish. He was aided by his father's influence and popularity, but had social gifts in his own right which, with his charming personality, alert mind, and somewhat dashing appearance, meant much. He grew from his origin and inheritance rather than being confined to them. He was educated in the Philadelphia schools,[1] which training he supplemented by a familiarity with the history and literature of his own and other countries through wide and steady reading.

Barker's literary and political activities were inaugurated at approximately the same time. He began his writing in 1804 with a three act play "with a marquis and a banditte in it."[2] This was based on Cervantes and entitled *The Spanish Rover*, only one act of which he completed. Two years later, when Barker hinted to Dunlap that he had composed a drama, referring to his mask *America*, he was advised to burn it, as first pieces were usually unfit for appearance. "When I got home, determined to obey the injunction of the oracle, I took up the mask with zeal to destroy. But no: I could not immolate liberty, science, peace, plenty—nay, my country *America*—and so I saved my conscience by bringing the *Spanish Rover*, robbers, and all, to the stake, a fate which I dare say they richly deserved."[3] *America*, this mask that so escaped the fire, was

1 Anon. biographical sketch, ms, Keys Collection, Baltimore.

2 William Dunlap, *History of the American Theatre*, pp. 376–380. This is a letter containing Barker's own account of his plays.

3 Dunlap, *op. cit.*, p. 377.

written in 1805. In it America, Liberty and Science engaged in political dialogue. There were attendant spirits and the whole was modeled on the mask in the *Tempest*.[4] It was intended as a conclusion to *The Indian Princess;* but that proving lengthy enough in itself, the mask was put aside. It has not survived.

The reading of Gibbon suggested another play at that time, a tragedy named *Attila*.[5] The better part of two acts were completed. A number of years later, about 1830, he was thinking of finishing the play for Forrest when he learned that Stone had an *Attila* almost ready for production. Others, too, had come upon the same theme, with the result that Barker's version remained incomplete. He had some affection for *Attila*, evidently, as he himself writes, " Should I ever be tempted to do anything more in the dramatic way, it will be to finish *Attila*. He is certainly an excellent stage personage." [6] This never occurred, and the two acts that were written have not come down to us.

Barker was anticipated in several other subjects he had under consideration for dramatic treatment at various times. Damon and Pythias as well as Wallace were among the heroes selected. He had even progressed so far as making a plot upon Epaminondas when Dr. Bird's play appeared—" half a dozen literary projects of mine have met a similar fate." [7]

In the spring of 1806 Barker attended a dinner at the club house of the Schuylkill Fishing Company where a discussion of Breck's *Fox Chase*, which had just been staged, led manager Warren to ask Barker to do a play and Jefferson to request a Yankee character for him to act.[8] *Tears and Smiles*, a comedy of Philadelphia manners, was the result. It was to be known as *Name it Yourself*, but that title was found to have been pre-

4 *Ibid.*, p. 376.
5 *Ibid.*, p. 376.
6 *Ibid.*, p. 376.
7 *Ibid.*, p. 377.
8 *Ibid.*, p. 377.

empted. The play is uneven in style but has a vivacity and a gleaming humor that help counterbalance some moral triteness and sentimental delinquencies. It reflects some of the contemporary interest in the Mediterranean pirates and takes a number of suggestions from Royall Tyler's *The Contrast*.[9]

The general pattern of the plot of *Tears and Smiles* is modeled on this older play. Sydney returns a hero from the successful campaign against the Mediterranean pirates to find Louisa Campdon about to marry a French fop, Fluttermore. After necessary complications involving the good offices of Widow Freegrace and her love affair with Rangely and the discovery of Sydney's parents, Sydney wins Louisa and Fluttermore is set in the path of a reformed and apparently virtuous life. All this, as in the plot of *The Contrast*, is subordinate to the satire on the manners of the day and to the characterization. The insincerity of social form, the undue influence of wealth and family, and the aping of foreign etiquette bear the brunt of the satire and are the source of much of the humor as are minor characters like Miss Starchington. Several of the more prominent of Barker's characters, further, are suggested by the older play. Sydney goes back to Colonel Manly, Nathan Yank is a descendant of Jonathan, while Fluttermore and Dimple are fops of similar breed. The main difference arises in the reflection of changed national prejudice through a substitution of imitation French fashions in Fluttermore for the second hand English ones of Dimple.

Tears and Smiles by way of the character of Nathan Yank leads through from the Yankee Jonathan to Woodworth's *The Forest Rose* and the Yankee plays of J. S. Jones and C. A. Logan that enjoyed great popularity years afterward. On the other hand it is a link in the development of social satire from *The Contrast* of Tyler and *The Father* by Dunlap to the work

9 A. H. Quinn, *Representative American Plays, New York,* 1917, contains a reprint of *The Contrast,* pp. 47–77.

of Mrs. Mowatt in *Fashion* of 1845 and so to the several imitations of that play.

Before *Tears and Smiles* was produced, Barker's interest was temporarily turned aside by other adventurous activity. In 1806 a certain General Miranda had agents in various cities of the United States to raise money and secure enlistments for an expedition to set up freedom in Venezuela and ultimately secure the independence of all South America.[10] Miranda was a picturesque character fond of display and splendid gesture. He was a native of Venezuela but had served in the French Army and taken part in the French Revolution. He made promises of most liberal pay and final wealth and fame to those who would take up this cause of independence. It was said that the United States government had given its implied sanction to the whole affair. There was much interest displayed all over the country. In February, 1806 Miranda sailed for Trinidad. Further efforts were made to form additional expeditions to join him. All through August of 1806 the Philadelphia *Aurora* contained notices of Miranda and appeals to " friends and countrymen "[11] in South America. Barker, following his inbred love for freedom and democracy and his natural ambition for the promised fame and glory, left home for New York early in August to sail to join the expedition in the West Indies. He had gone without his parents' consent—and on August 15 wrote to his father to explain his purpose and request approval of the project.[12] This, together with a letter that followed it the next day, shows the youthful enthusiasm and charming nature of Barker. He assumed as " my motto in life or in death ' make Honor your guide,' "[13] a precept his father had given him. The sailing was delayed and in the meanwhile news of Miranda's first disastrous

10 See James Biggs, *History of Don Francesca de Miranda's Attempt to Effect a Revolution in South America,* Boston, 1819, for a detailed account.

11 August 1, 1806.

12 Ms letter, August 16, 1806, Historical Society of Pennsylvania.

13 *Ibid.*

failure had arrived.[14] His father appealed to him to give up the whole idea.[15] Further report seemed to confirm the futility of Miranda's attempt. Whether young Barker gave up the adventure or not is obscure. These letters between father and son reveal the deep love they held for one another. They are couched in the over formal style of the day but behind the lines is the glow of truly chivalrous personalities.

Barker, at all events, had returned to Philadelphia in time to witness the premier performance of his first staged play, *Tears and Smiles*, given at the Chestnut Street Theatre, March 4, 1807.[16] Durang testifies to the play's decided success and great merit.[17] It was performed again on the following evening when an effort was made by " certain witlings about town " to break up the play by loud remarks from one of the boxes. Barker personally attended to the matter and " calling out one of the gentlemen, made such an expostulation as had the desired effect." [18] He gave the copyright to Blake who transferred it to Longworth and before long this play, together with the *Indian Princess*, was on sale at Matthew Carey's book shop.[19] April 2, 1808 saw a third production of *Tears and Smiles* and it was again staged for the benefit of charity on May 17, 1813.[20]

This era was a somewhat restless one in Barker's career. He seemed driven by an urge for travel and adventure. In July, 1807, he was once more in New York planning a New England tour [21] that immediately materialized. From Providence, R. I., came rumors of a duel between Barker and a Tom Swift.[22]

14 *Aurora*, August 25, 1806.

15 Ms letter, August 24, 1806, Historical Society of Pennsylvania.

16 Dunlap, *op. cit.*, p. 377.

17 Charles Durang, *The Philadelphia Stage*, 1st series, Chap. xli.

18 Dunlap, *op. cit.*, p. 378.

19 *Democratic Press*, adv., Nov. 9, 1808.

20 See the *Democratic Press* for these dates.

21 Ms letter, July 27, 1807, Keys collection, Baltimore.

22 Ms letter of J. E. Blake, Aug. 3, 1807, Ridgway Library.

Barker's easy ways with money, growing from his generosity, compelled him from time to time to borrow from friends, one of whom frankly wrote to him while on this trip, " Your conscription of Bank Notes, my dear James, will not, I fear, easily be cured—permit me to recommend particular attention on that head before the disease is without remedy—otherwise you may perhaps some time or other surely rue the neglect." [23] The requested loan, nevertheless, was enclosed, while the disease proved incurable.

The patriotic excitement over the difficulties between England and America and the resulting Embargo Bills of 1807 and 1808 was made use of by the actors of the time to increase the profits of their benefits. Blissett, partly for that reason, asked Barker to write a play for him based on the topics of the day,[24] which resulted in *The Embargo; or, What News?* put on at the Chestnut Street Theatre as part of Blissett's benefit, March 16, 1808.[25] A drama called *The Fortress* was played first that night and, as the advertisement read—" End of the Play, a New Interlude written by a Gentleman of this City." [26] It was, as Barker puts it " liberally borrowed from Murphy's *Upholsterer*.[27] As *The Embargo* was not printed and the manuscript has disappeared, the extent and nature of the adaptation of Murphy's play can only be gathered by a comparison of the partial caste as advertised for Barker's play with the characters in *The Upholsterer.*

Embargo [28]	*Upholsterer* [29]
Lieut. Hatchway	Quidnunc
Paragraph	Pamphlet
Tradewell	Razor
Whisper	Belmour

23 *Ibid.*

24 Durang, *op. cit.*, Chap. xli.

25 *Poulson's Advertiser,* Philadelphia, March 16, 1808.

26 *Democratic Press,* March 15, 1808.

27 Dunlap, *op. cit.,* p. 378.

28 *Freeman's Journal,* Philadelphia, March 16, 1808.

29 *Modern British Drama,* London, 1811, V, 439–452.

Hawser	Ronewell
Strop	Feeble
	Brisk
	Codicil

The similarity seems to have been close in general tone, but whether there was more specific imitation in action and phrasing cannot be determined. At any rate, Barker infused into his comedy popular Democratic sentiments of the day. "The subject of an embargo, then existing, was rather tickelish," he wrote, "and some of the patriotic sentiments were somewhat coldly received by a portion of the audience; but the majority were of the right feeling, and bore me triumphantly through. Very much to their credit, several of our merchants were distinguished for the applause they bestowed." [30] He further states that Blissett took the play to Baltimore, where it was produced, and then at Bernard's request sent it to Boston.

Sometime before this Barker had begun a play on the Pocahontas story, which he took up again in 1808; and at the suggestion of Bray, a composer, turned it into an operatic piece with songs set to music by Bray. It was called *The Indian Princess; or, La Belle Sauvage*, and was first staged for Bray's benefit at the Chestnut Street Theatre, April 6, 1808.[31] Webster, an Irishman, had the part of Larry. He had been the object of resentment and attack and on the night of the 6th the theatre was filled with belligerents determined either to support Webster or to drive him from the boards. A riot occurred, "the piece was not heard and the curtain fell on a rude commotion." [32] This led to press attacks upon the disorders in the theatre and startling comment on the rowdies gathering there.[33]

The theme of *The Indian Princess* was founded on the story of

[30] Dunlap, *op. cit.*, p. 378.

[31] *Democratic Press*, April 5, 1808.

[32] Durang, *op. cit.*, Chap. xli.

[33] *The Trangram*, Philadelphia, November 1, 1809; *Tickler*, Philadelphia, April 7, 1808.

Captain John Smith and Pocahontas taken from Smith's *General History of Virginia*,[34] 1624. The saving of the English is not, in the drama, the dominant interest but is overshadowed by the love theme presented through no fewer than five pairs of lovers in the persons of Pocahontas and Rolfe, Percy and Geraldine, Walter and Alice, Larry and Kate, and Robin and Pocahontas's maid, Nima. The characterization is adequate and these people are realized as individuals in most cases. Pocahontas, it is true, is somewhat stilted and over-poetical in thought and speech. The minor characters, as Walter, Larry, Robin or Alice are easier. They were entirely Barker's invention and carry the humour necessary to forward the play successfully. It was their omission that led to criticism of the play because of its want of comic relief when an altered version was staged in London.

Barker's use of historical material is in no way hampered by over-insistance upon accuracy of detail and chronology. He alters both when dramatic principle makes change desirable. The description of Virginia that largely makes up the first scene of Act I is derived with some closeness from the history.[35] The second and third scenes of that act, however, are mostly original. The news of Smith's departure on an exploring expedition in the one, and the Indian names of characters and places in the other [36] are the only contributions of Captain Smith. The fourth and main scene of this same Act I, that of Smith's fight with the Indians and his capture by Nantaquas, Pocahontas's brother, is historical in both character and incident [37] although the emphasis is shifted somewhat to give Nantaquas and his friendly attitude more prominence. The fifth scene, revolving about Rolfe, Percy and minor pairs of lovers, is invented. The opening scene of

34 Advertisement, *Indian Princess,* 1808 ed.

35 Captain John Smith, *The General History of Virginia* (London, 1624), p. 25.

36 *Ibid.,* pp. 27, 47, 50.

37 *Ibid.,* pp. 37, 51–52, 121.

Act II is that of Smith's dramatic rescue by Pocahontas, in which Barker parallels the historical account in general development [38] with readjustment of details that heightens the theatrical note. The meeting of Rolfe and Pocahontas in Sc. 2 grows out of a mere hint in Smith's narrative, as does the declaration of war by Powhatan on Miami's tribe in the next scene.[39] The humorous element furnished by Walter, Larry, Robin and Nima seems entirely Barker's and in characteristic vein. Sc. 1 of the third and last act is a blend, again, of fact and fiction. The alliance between Powhatan and the English with its subsequent success and some of the incidents in Walter's story of his voyage of discovery are derived; [40] while all other material of the scene is fictitious. In Sc. 2, Act III, the ideas concerning the instruction of Pocahontas, together with the influence of the Indian priests in warfare, are gathered from the *General History*.[41] The love of Pocahontas for Rolfe in this scene is portrayed in blank verse of unmistable excellence; and, although Indian utterance in such guise may appear extremely artificial, Pocahontas speaks with feeling and charm in the following able lines:

Princess: Wilt thou surely come?
Rolfe: To win thee from thy father will I come;
And my commander's voice shall join with mine,
To woo Powhatan to resign his treasure.
Princess: Go then, but ah! forget not—
Rolfe: I'll forget
All else to think on thee!
Princess: Thou art my life!
I lived not till I saw thee, love; and now,
I live not in thine absence. Long, O! long
I was the savage child of savage Nature;
And when her flowers sprang up, while each green bough

[38] *Ibid.*, pp. 54–55, 121.
[39] *Ibid.*, pp. 113, 39.
[40] *Ibid.*, p. 39.
[41] Pp. 116, 121, 39.

Sang with the passing west wind's rustling breath;
When her warm visitor, flush'd Summer, came,
Or Autumn strew'd her yellow leaves around,
Or the shrill north wind pip'd his mournful music,
I saw the changing brow of my wild mother
With neither love nor dread. But now, O! now,
I could entreat her for eternal smiles,
So thou might'st range through groves of loveliest flowers,
Where never Winter, with his icy lip,
Should dare to press thy cheek.

The arrival of the two women, mistress and maid, Pocahontas's warning of Powhatan's treachery and the coming of Lord Delaware in Sc. 3 are events recorded by Smith [42] but are considerably revised by Barker. The chronology especially is changed throughout, as Lord Delaware, for instance, did not arrive until 1610, three years after the time of the events in the play. The concluding scene of the banquet, the rescue of the English, and the happy disposition of the lovers is only a faint reflection of historical facts. A few quite indirect hints, if hints at all, give somewhat vague foundation for the banquet scene, the betrayal, and the arrival of Lord Delaware.[43] The patriotic vein of the final lines spoken by Smith is well in keeping with what must have been the spirit of *The Embargo* or the patriotism woven into the later *Marmion.*

While *Ponteach* of Robert Rogers, 1766, and Anne K. Hatton's *Tammany* of 1794 preceded *The Indian Princess* it was, as Professor Quinn points out,[44] the real beginning of the Indian drama and the first of several plays upon the Pocahontas story. This story was the theme of G. W. P. Custis's *Pocahontas, or the Settlers of Virginia* in 1830, of Robert D. Owens's *Pocahontas,* 1837; of *The Forest Princess* by Charlotte B. Conner, 1848, and of John Brougham's satire, *Pocahontas, or the*

42 *Ibid.,* pp. 75, 105, 81, 82, 121.

43 *Ibid.,* pp. 83, 86–87, 98.

44 *The American Drama from the Beginning to the Civil War,* p. 270.

Gentle Savage, that ended the series in 1855. It is estimated [45] that the plays on the general subject of the Indian numbered about forty during the years 1825–1860; hence Barker's inauguration of the Indian motive in 1808 was a fairly important event in American dramatic history.

The Indian Princess was produced again on February 1, 1809 [46] after having been advertised for January 25, 1809. It had its New York premier January 14, 1809, as a benefit for the English actress, Mrs. Lipman—" an American play actually produced in an American theatre, and for the benefit of an English actress " was, according to Odell, " an historic and thrilling event." [47] It was repeated in New York for Dunlap's benefit June 23, of that season,[48] and " it was to be many a long year before an American play would have a fair chance with an American audience in an American theatre." [49] Barker wrote, however, that it was frequently acted " in, I believe, all the theatres of the United States." [50]

It was on December 15, 1820,[51] at the Theatre Royal, Drury Lane, London that this same drama was the first original American play to receive a hearing in England after a premier production in America. Although Barker observes that from a critical sketch " this piece differs essentially from mine," [52] Genest definitely attributes it to him,[53] and the comment of the London *Times* and contemporary English magazines seems to support Barker's authorship. The situation illustrated the conditions in the theatrical world of the time. The actor Cooper, who brought

45 *Ibid.*, p. 275.

46 *United States Gazette,* Philadelphia, January 31, 1809.

47 G. C. D. Odell, *Annals of the New York Stage,* II, 318.

48 *Ibid.*

49 *Ibid.*

50 Dunlap, *op. cit.*, p. 379.

51 London *Times,* December 15, 1820.

52 Dunlap, *op. cit.*, p. 379.

53 John Genest, *Some Account of the English Stage, 1660–1830,* London, 1832, IX, pp. 83–84.

out the play in London, had played the title role in *Marmion*, had corresponded with Barker,[54] and had suggested that *Marmion* could be produced in London through his influence. Nothing was done at the moment, but at this later date without so much as a single " may I " he seems to have helped himself to *The Indian Princess*, after making alterations. The criticism of the London *Times* indicates something as to the changes in title, names, and comic parts. The notice of the verse and dominance of love theme point to Barker as does the comment upon the music attached. " Drury Lane Theatre. A drama in three acts, called *Pocahontas; or, the Indian Princess*, was performed at this theatre last night for the first time. The subject is borrowed from the early history of the English settlers in Virginia, and is not destitute in itself of the interest derived from the intercourse of civilized life with savage habits and manners. Love, the common bond and point of union in the human race, is the master key to the whole drama. *Pocahontas* saves the life of an English officer, who had indiscreetly ventured into the domains and becomes amenable to the laws of her royal father, and the reward of both in marriage. The outline of the piece is better than the execution: good situations are to be found in it; but the general conduct discovers little skill; while the want of comic characters communicates a leaden dullness which must prove a formidable barrier to a long and brilliant career. The dialogue is not deficient in harmony; but the speeches have one great and general fault—that of being too sentimental and didactic. Some music is attached to the piece, which is not without merit; and its value was not lessened by the skill and precision imparted by Miss Povey to her share in it. Cooper and Mrs. West were the hero and heroine; and the assistance of Booth's talents is also given. His character is that of an Indian chief, with a name (Opechancanough) not very easy to pronounce, and therefore, wisely enough, not once trusted to the metre. The writer, indeed, seemed in this respect very

[54] Ms letter, T. A. Cooper, February 16, 1812, Ridgway Library.

shy of his *dramatis personae,* a reserve that an inspection of the play-bill will easily account for. The announcement for repetition was not received with much ardour; but the 'contents' were predominant."[55] *The Gentleman's Magazine,* on the contrary, declared that it was "well acted and much applauded."[56] The writer for the *European Magazine and London Review* was somewhat satirical in comment. He reported "some slight hissing and loud applause" when the drama was announced for repetition, and gave the following cast:[57]

English Colonists

Captain Smith, President of the Colony, Mr. Cooper
Screvener, Vice-President, Foote
Ratcliffe and Archer, Members of the Council, Barnard and Bromley

Indians

Powhatan, Emperor of the Indians, Powell
Opechancanough, Tributary to Powhatan, Booth
Zapazan, Pope
Pocahontas, Daughter to Powhatan, Mrs. West
Monaca, Miss Povey
Creca, Miss Arbitt

It was pronounced unsuccessful by the *New Monthly Magazine* but praised for poetical qualities and dramatic skill in arrangement of scenes.[58] Its appeal was strong enough to secure for it two additional performances on December 16 and 19.[59] It was criticized for lack of humor and hopeless nomenclature, among other faults, all of which had been introduced through the revision of Barker's original work. This London production could not possibly have been the other likely American play on this theme—G. W. P. Custis's *Pocahontas*—as that did not ap-

55 London *Times,* December 17, 1820.
56 *The Gentleman's Magazine* (London, 1820), XL, 561.
57 LXXVII (December, 1820), 544.
58 III (January, 1821), 12.
59 London *Times,* December 16, 19, 1820.

pear until January 16, 1830,[60] while in 1820 the London production was said to be "an American Opera . . . yet to be found in all collections of the American stage." [61]

Barker's ill fortune with the production of his plays followed him in his adaptation of Cherry's *Travellers; or, Music's Fascination* that was announced for November 22, 1808.[62] Mr. Wilmot, who evidently was to have the main part, was afflicted with "indisposition," and the play was unavoidably postponed,[63] and then had to give way to an engagement of Cooper's. It finally had its day, December 26, 1808, being advertised as "altered and adapted to the American stage by a citizen of Philadelphia. . . . The Scenery, Machinery, Dresses and Decorations *nearly* new." [64] Barker had Americanized the play at the request of the managers "making it, I am afraid, little less absurd than I found it." [65] However, it was a success, being, as Durang points out, tastefully and very cleverly altered and successfully placed before the public.[66] It was repeated December 30, 1808,[67] and January 21, 1809.[68] The play has not been preserved, but in the theatrical advertisements the fifth act, as the only one mentioned, appears to have been the main attraction in Barker's version. "Act 5—America—The stage is found to represent the Quarter Deck of an American Frigate." Those on board are Commodore Hawser, Ben Buntline, Midshipman Mast F, and Sailors.[69] According to the notice for the original play as given in 1807 the acts were: I China, II Turkey, III and

60 A. H. Quinn, *History of the American Drama,* p. 272.

61 *European Magazine,* LXXVIII (December, 1820), 544.

62 *Poulson's Advertiser,* November 21, 1808.

63 *Ibid.*

64 *Ibid.,* December 26, 1808.

65 Dunlap, *op. cit.,* p. 379.

66 Durang, *op. cit.,* Chap. xlii.

67 *Poulson's Advertiser,* December 30, 1808.

68 *United States Gazette,* January 21, 1809.

69 *Ibid.*

IV Italy, V Main deck of a man of war.[70] In view of the changes suggested by Act V, the alterations were fairly extensive. The use of Cherry's name might merely indicate the usual derogatory attitude toward native playwrights.

Dramatic activity had not, during this period, absorbed the whole of Barker's interest. By September of 1808, he had become active in the Philadelphia political organization known as "The Democratic Young Men" [71] and July 4, 1809, he combined his literary and political enthusiasms by composing a song sung at that organization's celebration of the day. It was without definite name, simply being headed "song." In the first stanza he strikes a mood expressive of his characteristic Americanism. It is uninspired, but spirited, with a somewhat catching lilt and runs:

Ye patriots of Columbia
Who prize the honor'd name;
Ye heroes of her future wars,
And guardians of her fame,
Oh hail with songs of joy, the day,
When first she dar'd be free,
While around, swell'd the sound,
Of the voice of Liberty—
When the Clarion's breath, that call'd to death,
Was the voice of Liberty.[72]

The second stanza eulogizes the fathers of the Revolution, the third "scorns the boast of birth," while the last is a rallying cry for believers in the freedom of the sea.

His patriotism was given some practical experience when that fall at a meeting of the "Democratic Young Men" he was named a member of a committee of vigilance to supervise the vot-

70 *Aurora,* April 18, 1807.
71 *Democratic Press,* September 23, 1808.
72 *Ibid.,* July 7, 1809.

ing at the election that resulted in Democratic control of councils and so led in his father's second term as mayor of the city.[73]

December 21, 1809,[74] Barker arrived in Washington armed with letters of introduction to his father's friend, James Madison, and numerous other government officials, who proved most anxious to keep on amiable terms with the fiery old Democrat in political control in Philadelphia. The visit evidently had a two-fold purpose—to give the younger Barker social contacts and valuable friends, in the first place; and to offer him an opportunity, in the second place, to inform himself politically at the fountain head, observe governmental procedure, and generally train himself for a political future. The visit was, too, still another phase of his uneasy seeking for adventure and a career. The eleven letters addressed to his father covering the duration of his stay from December 21, 1809, to the close of March, 1810 (the last letter is undated), not only throw much light upon Washington society and politics of the day, but rather intimately portray Barker's tastes, moods, and judgments. The affectionate, if slightly formal, attitude of father and son adds other charm to both their characters. The style is pointed and surprisingly direct in that age of elaborate, set English, ceremonial salutations, and epistolary indirection. Their interpretative value and intrinsic interest give them importance. They are here reproduced in full.

WASHINGTON, 21 Dec., 1809.

Dear Father;

I write simply to inform you of my safe arrival here after spending one day in Baltimore. I have seen Dr. Seybert[75] but have not yet presented my other letters. The debate on Giles'[76] resolutions

73 *Ibid.,* October 6, 1809.

74 Ms letter, December 21, 1809, Keys collection, Baltimore.

75 Adam Seybert, Representative from Pennsylvania.

76 W. B. Giles, Senator from Virginia. The resolutions originated in his committee in the Senate and grew out of the portion of Pres. Madison's message concerning foreign affairs.

employs the House Repr. at present. I have heard Dana [77] and several others. Quincy [78] and many more are to speak yet. The resolutions will no doubt pass—at the close of the week. It is twelve o'clock and the " Spouters have met ". I close abruptly. I will take the pleasure to write in one or two days.

Yr. Affec. Son

Jas. N. Barker

J. Barker, Esq.

Washington, 27 Dec., 1809.

Dear Sir;

Entertaining the idea that I should be enabled to furnish you with some news, I have delayed writing for some days past. Affairs, however, not appearing likely to change their aspect, I take advantage of a private hand to forward you a very hasty sketch—hasty by necessity, for every moment of my time is engaged.

I have heard enough speeches to fill half a dozen volumes, but not a spice of eloquence till to day when Mr. Eppes [79] made what is termed the administration speech. It will be some days before you see it; in the meantime you may be assured it is the very best that has been or will be delivered. Messers Dana—Emott [80] and Gold [81] writhed under his lash and almost literally were whipt from their seats.

The committee of the whole rose to day and will not, it is supposed sit again. A motion for indefinite postponement of the consideration of the resolution was made by Livermore [82] and supported by his oratory and his colleagues' votes, but was lost. Meanwhile the speeches go on, and probably next week will scarcely see an end of them. I shall thus have the opportunity of hearing *every member* who has the least pretension to speaking. It is impossible to say what will be the end of all this. The resolutions will certainly pass; but nothing else is certain, except that they will pass under

[77] S. W. Dana, Representative from Connecticut.

[78] Josiah Quincy, Representative from Massachusetts.

[79] J. W. Eppes, Representative from Virginia.

[80] James Emott, Representative from New York.

[81] T. R. Gold, Representative from New York.

[82] Edward Livermore, Representative from Massachusetts.

such a load of verbiage and rubbish as must prevent any good effect which they might under other circumstances, (a silent and unanimous vote, for instance) have had. You would have a pain at heart to be a week near the capitol,—only to be eased by laughing at Folly. In fact, Inveterate Toryism, indecision, and I may add, ignorance form the characteristicks of our Congress. Every Member out of doors, knows this and complains of his neighbour and yet every one in the house unites in pursuing the same plan traced by imbecility, and ideotism. The capitol Sir (I speak figuratively, for literally it is a superb building) is like a scene in the playhouse very well at a distance, but rough, rude and disgusting at a near view. I should like to declaim on this theme, and following the illustrious examples in the house, use it as they do Giles' resolutions—that is make it a starting place to branch out from into more ramifications than there are avenues from the Capitol—I will defer this and many other things, however, for the present and indeed I ought to beg your pardon for scrawling at all just now: for the truth is, I have just broke loose from Mr. Taylor's [83] table. Lieutenant Reed and myself dined with him to day together with his lady—Mr. and Mrs. Marion [84]—Governor Fenner [85]—Macon [86]—Bibb [87] and a whole tribe of the luminaries. Dr. Seybert has made me known to at least 50 of the house some of whom recollect you with respect as Messrs. Smilie,[88] Findley [89] etc. and I am known to almost all the members on one side and to several on the other. Mrs. and Mr. Gallatin [90] entertained me with very gratifying civilities. I am to be presented to the President to morrow and shall go to his Lady's drawing room in the evening. On Newyearsday there will be a grand Levee which I shall attend. My time is very agreeably passed, nay I have not half enough of it. I ate my Christmas turkey at the great [illegible] Falls of the Potomac 15 miles from the city. Thirty-two

83 Likely John Taylor, Representative from South Carolina.

84 Robert Marion, Representative from South Carolina.

85 James Fenner, Governor of Rhode Island.

86 Nathaniel Macon, Representative from North Carolina.

87 W. W. Bibb, Representative from Georgia.

88 John Smilie, Representative from Pennsylvania.

89 William Findley, Representative from Pennsylvania.

90 Albert Gallatin, Secretary of the Treasury.

miles on horseback was a great days journey for me, but the sight fully compensated the trouble. The capital and the Presidents' house are more suberb than any thing I had conceived of, and the rest of the place more wretched. Dr. Leib [91] was with Dr. Seybert when I met him first, and in pursuance of your instructions I couldn't forbear meeting his hand when I saw it held out with a smile. He [hoped] I had left *my friends* well.

Before I close, I must again apologise for scribbling just now, but upon my word I have no other time, and even now occupy one end of a supper table, while others are eating. In the morning before the House meet, I pay my visits. Some orator or other always keeps the floor till 4 o'clock and it is dark at 5—I will write very soon. Meanwhile I pay you the compliments of the season and hope you may have many Christmasses as happy as my last. Extend this to Molly—to Hester and all, and believe me

Yr. Affect. Son

JAMES N. BARKER.

WASHINGTON, 29th Dec., 1809.

Dear Father;

Yesterday morning I was presented to the President by Dr. Seybert accompanied by Mr. Sawyer.[92] The awe necessarily inspired by the occasion and place was immediately dispelled by the courteous deportment of our worthy chief magistrate; and the few minutes which propriety restricts us to in interviews of this kind, were passed in a manner very gratifying to my feelings personal and filial. His inquiries after your health, and pleasure in hearing you were well, were not only polite; they were cordial. I dined with Dr. S. and a very large and elegant party—Tea brought us an accession. There were Judge Thurston [93] and Lady, Mr. and Mrs. Poindexter; [94] a charming girl from Alexandria—P. M. Randolph [95]—Sawyer—

91 Michael Leib, Senator from Pennsylvania, a bitter opponent of John Barker.

92 Lemuel Sawyer, Representative from North Carolina.

93 Buckner Thurston, United States Judge of District Court.

94 George Poindexter, Representative from Mississippi Territory.

95 Likely I. M. Randolph, former Congressman from Virginia.

Milnor,[96] Johnson,[97] Livingston,[98] and twenty others. In the evening the tea room was converted into a ball room, the judge was our fidler and we danced till we were tired. My time flies on the wings of pleasure. I attend the ladies to the Capitol in the morning—dine with some agreeable party and end the evening with singing or dancing among sages and senators and their wives and daughters. 'Tis a fine field this for the Study of Human character. The Capitoline Hill is a focus that unites rays (whether brilliant or not!) from every point of our Hemisphere. Every peculiarity—every dialect of our extensive and various country is (I hope not unprofitiably.) seen and listened to.

The debate on the resolutions seems drawing to an end. Indeed it must close soon for almost every member has spoken, some, twice, and they dare not speak oftener. Quincy concluded to day, reading a speech begun yesterday, in which, to use a cant congressional phase—he *smashed!* that is—he lost himself in his volume of notes—feigned illness, and sat down. The laugh was universal through the city at the expense of the would be orator, and his situation was compared to that of the man in the play, from whose hat a wag steals his fine set speech, and forces him to finish with " I want words—I want words—upon my soul I want words." In the course of last evening, I made some mirth and perhaps was fortunate enough to introduce a new word into the cant vocabularly.—We had been very merry with the short hand orator on someone asking me to sing a song which I knew but imperfectly I couldn't help expressing my fears that as I hadn't *the notes,* I should be obliged to *Quincy* in the midst! I was *bravo'd* from every corner—for you'll please to recollect we were all Democrats, man, woman and child—you'll be good enough also to pardon [this] piece of egotism, and my careless mode of writing—I should be unhappy indeed, did my spirits carry me beyond the limits of respect and duty.

My next shall not, if I can help it, be such a scribble-scrabble—

Affectionately yours

P. S. Respects to all. JAMES N. BARKER

[96] William Milnor, Representative from Pennsylvania.

[97] R. M. Johnson, Representative from Kentucky.

[98] R. L. Livingston, Representative from New York.

WASHINGTON, 3 Jany., 1810.

Dear Father;

Giles' resolutions still occupy the House. Last night Livermore closed a speech tiresome as it was long. He was frequently interrupted by his friends who called for an adjournment, but the Democrats intending to close the question of indefinite postponement wouldn't agree to let him break off, to resume in the morning. The question was finally taken and of course lost. The question on the passage of the resolutions still remains under discussion and will for some time. More fuss has certainly been made on the subject than it deserved. After all will not the President be placed in a delicate situation when resolutions approbating of his own conduct are presented to him for his signature, I think (with a great many members here, in private by the way) they were ill contrived. The knowing ones, however, whisper of amends being made by something more efficient soon coming out, to originate in the Senate. I myself know that a member of the House has *in petto* a most flaming string of resolves. The majority can do any thing, isn't it surprising that they don't do some thing? . . . I really believe (and perhaps the idea is as erroneous as original) that the wildness of the place (city called by courtesy) serves to deaden the spirit of legislation. The bustle of a city *like a city*, produces activity of mind—more especially when we see around us thousands of those persons whom we are to take care of. Here, as legislation sees no immediate object but clods of dirt, the representative is as heavy as the apparent constitu[ent].

If the splendour of one house (the palace) were divided and distributed it would produce elegance in a thousand. On Monday, there was a grand Levee—I bowed among the rest—I was highly delighted with the scene. A suit of 4 rooms was open and all thronged. The heads of departments, foreign ministers &c. and all the gentry of the vicinage attended of course.

I break off abruptly—to run to the House. Dr. Seybert's attention is unremitting. I meet with civilities on every hand, but I have not yet heard from Philad--. How comes it?

Adieu Dear Sir

Your Aff. Son

John Barker, Esq. JAMES N. BARKER

WASHINGTON, 10 Jany., 1810.

Dear Father;

A duel took place this day at 12 o'clock between Capt. Gordon of the brig Siren, and Hanson the Tory Editor of Baltimore. Gordon was brought to our hotel, it is supposed mortally wounded. I have just left his room. His agony is extreme. The quarrel was originally between Hanson and the son of Gov. Wright [99]—Gordon was employed as Wright's friend to bear a challenge to Hanson, who refused to fight the Governor, but intimated his willingness to meet any one who chose to take his place. Gordon instantly took it. After all Hanson was very averse to fighting—(like most of his brother editors) but couldn't possibly avoid it.—My room is precisely over the wounded man's. I hear him groaning at this moment.

11th Instant.

I am infinitely happy to say that from several favorable symptoms, the doctors have hope of Gordon's recovery. He passed a fine night and this morning conversed freely. He, it appears, did not fire, but reserved his ball, as he says, to send it cooly to the heart of Hanson, and thus rid his country and the world of a damned Englishman, those were his words. *Gallatin* who lives just opposite us, has had him removed to his house in a litter. J. G. Jackson [100] is almost well—he dined yesterday at the Presidents'.

I was last night at the drawing room. Nothing can be more suberb. I much doubt whether any Queen in Europe is more elegant in every particular than our Lady of the palace. The President is very well, but hasn't the *manner* so perfectly—I was charmed with everything I saw. You see by the papers what Congress are doing—On Tuesday Seybert made his maiden speech. It pleased very generally. He hopes it will please you. He and several other democrats are opposed to the Bill.[101] It will, however, pass.—I heard Madison last night express his opinion of it, and if I recollect rightly, he thinks it too weak. I don't know how to leave this place for I have got into the most agreeable—*coterie* that can exist—I am

99 Robert Wright, Governor of Maryland.

100 Representative from Virginia.

101 "Respecting the commercial intercourse between the United States and Great Britain and France."

happy that Molly's *accouchment* has been favorable and I bestow my benediction on my little namesake. I quit my pen to dress for an assembly. In haste dear father

Your Affect. Son

John Barker, Esq. JAMES N. BARKER

Saturday, 13th.

No opportunity to send a letter offering, and I not having time to make one has kept this back thus long. Young Dr. Jackson's return to Philadelphia gives me the facility which my numerous avocations (pleasures) denied.

I have just left Mrs. Gallatin after an agreeable chat of an hour. Capt. Gordon has experienced many changes: the crisis will be to day. Very small hopes are entertained of his recovery. Young Wright is here and vows vengeance against Hanson. Thursday I was at a most brilliant Assembly. The Pres. and Lady and family, Secy. of State and family, Mansfield and wife—Tunneau and son, in fine all the Gentry attended. Mrs. Madison converses with me absolutely as if we had been acquainted 20 years. Every one loves her—a finer woman cannot live. Last night I was at a private party and saw a number of new faces. Moderately speaking, I have made a hundred or two of acquaintances, and I hope a few friends. I go to day to Alexandria as attendant cavalier of a Young Lady and her Mama of that place. My business increases so rapidly that I shant know when I shall be able to leave it. I am desired to give you respects from all quarters, but want room to particularise.

Unfeignedly Your Afft. Son

J. N. BARKER

WASHINGTON CITY, Jany. 14, 1810.

Dear Father;

I accompany this with a speech of Mr. Poindexter which I hope will be acceptable. Mr. and Mrs. P. are the most amiable people I know. She is at this moment expressing her pleasure in cutting and folding a pamphlet for so good a Democrat as Gen'l. Barker.

The House proceeds in its system of talking—Macons' [102] bill is

[102] A bill on commercial relations between the United States and Great Britain.

now before it and will finally pass. Sawyer intends this day proposing a new section, granting convoy &c. Burwell[103] will also offer an amendment granting letters of Marque &c. or else produce a new project.

I sometimes see the Aurora and find that Congress is no more liked with you than it is here in fact people dont hesitate to say it will be the last congress that will sit.

Last Wedy. at the drawing room I was introduced to Sec'y. Smith,[104] Eppes, Jackson &c., &c. I forgot to mention to you that I did not present H's letter to Smith. I can never think of giving a *sealed* letter from one who don't know me to a stranger of such precise manners as Gen'l. Smith. I have felt no loss by it, however, his daughter and niece I meet with in all companies.

The President's Message will at last produce nothing. Sec'y. Smith says that no volunteers will be raised. By the way, he and Gallatin are about at daggers drawn. He calls the last report of Gallatin a *vapid* production &c.

The other day there was a grand parade of the Marine Corps. I dined with the officers in mess—and was afterward taken all through the navy yard by the commandant, Capt. Carson. The monument to the memory of the Tripolitan Heroes is a very fine one.

It has been warm here till to day and now 'tis as cold as I ever felt it. Nevertheless I shall venture on a party (perhaps by water) to Alexandria, where there is an Assembly to night: from thence I shall proceed to Mount Vernon and on my return (unless I find a letter from you authorising and enabling me to stay longer in this land of delight) turn my head Philadelphia-ward

In the hope and expectation of a letter from you by return of post. I am, dear father

Yr. Affe. Son

J. N. Barker

John Barker, Esq.

P.S. Gordon is pronounced out of danger.

103 W. A. Burwell, Representative from Virginia.

104 Robert Smith, Secretary of State.

WASHINGTON, 9th Feby., 1810.

Dear Father;

I had the pleasure three days ago to receive your letter of the 1st. with the enclosure, than which nothing could come more opportunely. I shall assuredly take your advice to be as frugal as I can, the place, however, calls for frequent disbursements. The late snow has been productive of a novel pleasure and consequently new expenses.

Nothing of importance has occurred here lately. I am afraid Macons' Bill will pass the Senate—several however of that body expect otherwise. The Supreme Court is now sitting. We have Marshall, Washington and the other Judges at our house. Several lawyers from Philadelphia are here: Mr. C. Ingersoll, Hopkinson, Lewis &c.

Will obey your command of not returning till I hear from you and will depend on your promise not to forget me. I am dear father

Affectionately Your Son

J. N. BARKER

John Barker, Esq.

WASHINGTON, 1 March—10.

Dearest Sir;

I have been anxiously waiting to hear from you, exactly one month; your last was of the 1st. of Feby. I have written several times since and am afraid my disappointments have arisen from miscarriage of letters. I should be very grateful for such a reply to this as might enable me to quit my lodgings the next week. I wish it very particularly. The roads are fine and the weather fine and I should like to take a trip to Norfolk—or Annapolis or Fredericktown or some other place for a time. I am more than ever conscious of the trouble and expense which you incur from my vagaries and am more than ever determined one way or the other that they shall immediately cease. When I say that the pecuniary part of my obligation shall be discharged I only say what I am resolved to do, however trite the repetition has become. My other debts to you are as difficult to be paid as my sense of them is to be expressed. Both are impossible.

Macon's Bill, as you perceived, returned maimed from the Senate.

It was supposed the cripple would die on its journeys between the two houses. Eppes however, has given it a crutch which I hope will bear it stiffly up. Eppes is a noble fellow. His additional sections may be considered rather as a substitute for it than amendments to it. The Bill is just as imbecile as its author. Macon is invariably wrong.

Fulton's [105] torpedoes have not yet exploded. The Federalists have damped the powder—as they would damp the spirit of the nation.

I was present at an oration on the Birthday at Alexandria. R. G. Harper [106] libelled the shade of Washington and disgraced the day of his nativity.

Frugality is a virtue very difficult to be practised here. Boarding is 10$ a week and the article of hack-hire (indispensible every day and night) would keep a small family in Phila.—You will readily conceive my necessity for supplies. I hope you may be as well aware of my repugnance in applying. Your goodness is never exercised but with liberality. I need not therefore be specific. Be pleased to mention me to all my friends, and accept the unfeigned tender of affection

Your son

J. N. Barker

P.S. I would recommend as the safest conveyance of money a cover to Dr. Seybert.

2nd March.

It is said that John Randolph [107] arrived last night. This is the most variable climate for we have had the dead of winter and summer fifty times. Even today the morning was as delightful as possible—at noon there was a storm of thunder and lightening and now there is a storm of snow and rain—

Washington, 3 March,—10.

Dear Father;

Dr. Seybert handed me your favor of 25th. last evening just

105 Robert Fulton, inventor of the torpedo, steam boat, etc.

106 Former Congressman from South Carolina and a lawyer in Baltimore in 1810.

107 Representative from Virginia.

after I had dispatched mine of yesterday to the office—I have not yet had an opportunity of reading the proceedings—I had previously perused the address and resolutions [108] in the Aurora.[109] What does Duane's [110] refusal to publish the address to the people proceed from? Is the excuse he offers the true one—its false constructions?—I have not seen the Press.[111] Since I have been here, the Aurora is generally read. How do you stand with those two Grand Belligerents Duane and Binns? [112] It is impossible for a neutral to sail the sea of politics for them and a dignified retirement I should conceive most eligible.

The committee to whom was referred the lame Bill with Eppe's amendments will report on Monday, I expect, and will bring in Eppe's sections alone, modeled into a new bill.

There is a general buzz of expectation of John Randolph's arrival. He was seen on the road from Richmond. I wish he would come. The Torpedoe Bill [113] passed the Senate yesterday. Mrs. Hamilton's claim too has been allowed. The democratic party has gained credit for their liberality. Taylor, Johnson &c. distinguished themselves. Macon, as usual, opposed it. This Macon is a *rara avis.* If a question should arise in the House whether two and two made four, he, from the simple circumstance of the thing being self-evident would vote in the negative. His self sufficiency will never let him agree with any one. I will one day or other endeavour to sketch the characters of both houses for my amusement—if it amuses you also, I shall be happy.

How strange that I should forget Bennett's family. I visited them once—a month ago—and shall confess it—totally forgot them

108 These grew out of a Town Meeting called by John Barker, then Mayor of Philadelphia.

109 *Aurora,* a Philadelphia newspaper supporting the anti-administration faction of the democrats.

110 William Duane, editor of the *Aurora.*

111 *Democratic Press,* a Philadelphia newspaper supporting the administration.

112 John Binns, editor of the *Democratic Press.*

113 A bill appropriating $5,000 " for the purpose of trying the practical use of the torpedo, or sub-marine explosion."

since—They were not in the sphere of my motion. Bennett is doing well.

One inducement for my wish to leave W—is the intolerable expense.—A period of 3 months since my arrival here, will soon be completed.—At this moment I am on the book for $150—I am frightened to see how I go on. I am turning a thousand projects in my mind. Fortune hunting presents itself in various shapes. I cannot think with any patience of coming home so much poorer than I went away.

Yr. Affc. Son

J. N. Barker.

Shall I request you to fold your letters with a little more caution? Women are very curious and will peep. Dr. S. knew I would call last night, and being obliged to go out left your favor on the mantlepiece. I met him at the door and we went in together. One of the ladies had the letter in her hand but vowed she was only studying what the N of my address could stand for. I told her it stood for "Never *peep*."

Washington, 12 Ma. 10—

Dear Father;

I hasten to acknowledge the receipt of your favor enclosing the $200. In this instance, as in every other, I feel grateful for your kindness and liberality. My expenses have been, I know, enormous but indeed they were indispensebly incurred. I have not only been moving in the gayest circle of this most exorbitant of all cities—but have been necessarily whirled by the wheel of fashionable dissipation through all the gaieties of Alexandria and Georgetown. However 'tis time certainly, full time that the career should close—I hope two or three days will make no essential difference. John Randolph has been here and is supposed to have been preparing himself—during the present week, for making his *debut,* in the next when some animated discussion will assuredly take place. I have no intention of staying the whole week but feel almost confident you will have no objection to my remaining till Monday or perhaps Tuesday—to hear this great phenomenon of eloquence. Barnum was totally forgotten but it is now too late for recollection to be in time. He will certainly not be very difficult.

After all I think my money and time have not been wasted. I have bought much pleasure and I think useful friends.

Yr. obliged and affect. Son

J. N. BARKER

WASHINGTON [n. d.]

Dear Father;

This will be handed you by Mr. Taylor, the brother of the gentleman to whom Mr. Read was so polite as to give me a letter. He goes to Philadelphia to study under Dr. Barton.[114] I need not ask your attention for him.

I think the date of my last was the 9th, since which nothing particular has occurred. Mr. Fulton and his torpedoes engage present notice. He experimentises tomorrow at the Navy Yard.

I find you are making strenuous exertions in Philadelphia:[115] it is more than they do here. Nothing I am afraid but actual invasion can arouse our guardians from their torpor. They talk indeed, but they talk in their sleep, without correspondent action. The capitol is a parliament travestied, and debate is in inverse proportion to the importance of the subject matter. I much doubt whether there be knavery in Congress, for never was folly so universally visible and the two you know are incompatible. I dined with *Macon* &c., &c. to day and have no reason to change my opinion—Macon is an honest man but as far from a wise one as I am from a rich one. His bill however *will not pass the Senate* I firmly believe, and my belief is founded on that of (I could almost say) a majority of that body.—

I shall see by the papers what will be the result of your meeting. I fear that State politics will ruin its effect. Neither Simon Snyder[116] nor Conrad Weiser[117] should have anything to do with it. An appeal should be made to the Senate from all parts of the Union and that appeal should have but a single object. The salvation of the people rests with themselves: the habits of their representatives

114 Dr. Benjamin S. Barton, botanist and professor in the Medical School of the University of Pennsylvania.

115 This refers to his father's activity in arousing popular feeling in support of the President.

116 Governor of Pennsylvania.

117 A Pennsylvania politician.

are fixed. Indolence and inactivity or vain babbling are their characteristicks. The best braced minds have lost their tone, for the eternal cavils that are stated to the plainest business; the obstacles that are thrown in the way at every step of legislation—have at length wearied her out: she halts and the word of command must be given by the *General Will,* by the *Sovereign People,* before she can march. Is it not strange? There is a majority in Congress which could do anything, and they do nothing. A minority governs. Absolutely governs by quibble and quirks by hems and has.—They have been called a Spartan Band; they are so—greater than that at Thermopylae. I never enter the walls of the Capitol but I think of a little impish dwarf laughing in the face of a great lubberly giant or Gulliver tied down by a single Lilliputian. The truth is they want a leader. What would be the fate of an army were its general cut out into corporals? This is the case with Congress—a little, but compacted body over a huge army, for that army has no leader but in his place some score or two of *mis*leaders—each leading a different rout. Let the voice of the people say 'On'!—what did a small section of the Union do?—and what may not the whole do?—The first frightened a Majority—Cannot the latter awe a Minority?—If you think I am becoming a wiser man or a better patriot for remaining here, I am afraid you will be mistaken. Patriotism is here a stale jest and wisdom is a nonentity.

Forgive me if I turn from politicks to pleasure. The latter I do receive, but if within the Capitol at all, only from the gallery in which the ladies are seated. I mingle in an endless round of amusements [Two sentences follow but are illegible because of partial destruction of the page.]

I am, dear father,
Yr. most affect. Son
J. N. Barker.

P.S. Young Taylor does not go for some days. I therefore send this. Fulton Saturday lectured before a large company, on torpedoes; and made a powerful appeal to the mind.

Several of the characteristics and of the facts present in this correspondence attach significantly to Barker's personality and future experiences. The flares of humor are not only similar to those flashing in his plays but are indicative of certain cheerful aspects of his attitude in political life as well. His impatience with the slow pace of befuddled affairs in Washington is part of his ingrained love for decisive action. His belief, also, in the stimulating power of urban life bears on later interests and various activities in Philadelphia. The restlessness, further, under a sense of obligation belongs to his general independence, while the appreciation of his debt to his father comes from his chivalrous character. The promised endeavor to sketch some of the figures in public life for his own amusement may have been the germ of an idea that some seven years afterward bore results in his biographical writing for *Delaplaines Repository*. The evident interest in Fulton, likewise, led to a later sketch of his career and years after that to a leading share in relieving Fulton's distressed family. The aggressive tone of the comments upon national affairs is of the same patriotic spirit that motivated Barker's service in the War of 1812 and his tireless political activity in subsequent years.

On the return to Philadelphia, which must have occurred almost immediately after this last letter, it is probable that Barker for a time was engaged as his father's secretary, for several of John Barker's official communications appear to be in the son's handwriting. This would have been in keeping with the idea of training for public life and invaluable experience for him when in later days he himself became mayor of Philadelphia.

Barker's marriage seems to have taken place in 1811. His wife was Mary Rogers, who had come to Philadelphia from Lempster, N. H., with her sister and her brother Edmund, who was a portrait painter of some note.[118] The Rogers family was descended from Sir John Fitz Roger of Dorset, England, and Elizabeth Ferneaux, descendant of the Earls of Bush. The

118 J. S. Rogers, *James Rogers of New London Ct., and His Descendants,* Boston, 1902, p. 234.

first to come to America was James Rogers, who left England in 1635 and settled at New London, Connecticut, about 1656. James Rogers, the father of Mrs. Barker, was of the sixth generation. Her portrait by Thomas Sully,[119] painted at the close of 1827, shows her as a woman of unusual beauty,[120] as does the testimony of contemporaries.[121] It was perhaps from his brother-in-law that Barker acquired his knowledge and interest in painting. At one time he took up portrait painting, as an enthusiastic amateur, painting several pictures of his children [122] with a success that must have required considerable experience. He later in life gathered a collection of engravings that was the source of much pleasure, reflecting an interest again likely originating in Edmund Rogers. The Rogers family had come to Philadelphia, it would seem, as the most promising city for the artistic career of the brother. He ended as inspector of customs.

119 Account Book of Pictures Painted by T. Sully, ms under date December 12, 1827, Historical Society of Pennsylvania.

120 This together with another portrait of her and one of J. N. Barker, said to be by Rembrandt Peale, is in the possession of Miss Josephine Keys of Baltimore, the granddaughter.

121 Ms letter of Jacob Vogdes, March 8, 1810, Ridgway Library.

122 Keys Collection, Baltimore.

IV

MARMION AND THE WAR OF 1812

EARLY in 1812, a few months before his patriotism and loyalty carried him into active military service in the War of 1812, Barker completed the drama *Marmion*.[1] A good deal of the writing of it had been done during the winter of 1811 and had been undertaken at "the special request of Wood,"[2] the Philadelphia manager. This play was a dramatization of Scott's *Marmion* and proved to have the longest stage life of any of Barker's dramas. Here once more Barker had the experience of anticipation that had been his fate in several other instances. On the very same day that *Marmion* was sent off to New York for its first staging, Barker received a note from a Mrs. Ellis, asking him to give a few newspaper puffs to a play she was producing at the Olympic Theatre, Philadelphia, called *Marmion*.[3] This lady was the mother of a then popular actress of that name and had furnished the Olympic with other pieces. "By great diligence," as Durang phrases it, Mrs. Ellis "succeeded in bringing out her version of *Marmion* before James N. Barker could produce it at the Chestnut."[4] The Ellis version was performed at the Olympic March 30, and April 1, 3, and 4.[5] This anticipation may be a partial explanation for the opening of Barker's *Marmion* in New York and the presentation of it as of English composition. Barker and Manager Wood must have known of Mrs. Ellis's intention long before her note begging Barker's approval.

1 Dunlap, *op. cit.*, p. 379.

2 *Ibid.*

3 *Ibid.*

4 Durang, *op. cit.*, chap. xlviii.

5 See *Aurora* files for these dates.

The actor T. A. Cooper had the title role in the New York production and in a letter to Barker indicates the ruse by which it was played there as of English origin. He wrote in part "I am anxiously expecting the copy of M. as I have found it necessary to inform my painter that I have already *received the letter* announcing its arrival in a late vessel from Liverpool. This I have been obliged to do in order to get ready with the scenery. My request is that you write by return of post [and] if possible furnish me with the plot (description of scenes) that I may give it to Mr. Holland. I make some excuse for not giving him the book to read. He can immediately proceed. . . . You had better transmit the [manuscript] by Mr. Wood's means for obvious reasons and it should be well sealed—with a particular request that the delay of an hour may not unnecessarily take place." [6] Cooper announced the play as by Thomas Morton, the English playwright, and the first performance occurred, in the Park Theatre, New York, April 13, 1812, with much spectacle and scenery and an excellent cast. It was repeated there six times in a successful run of performances.[7] Barker, although pleased at the success, never felt very proud of the fraud.

As early as September 29, 1812, *Marmion* was advertised as being in preparation at the Chestnut Street Theatre, Philadelphia, where "the most splendid preparations are now making." [8] It was further heralded for a week in October and November, while by December 15 "The New Grand Tragedy of Marmion is nearly ready for representation." [9] It was finally scheduled for performance January 1, 1813, and had its Philadelphia premier that night. A modified form of the same deception that had been effective in New York was again used according to the following account of Manager Wood. "We insinuated that the piece was a London one, had it sent to our theatre from New

6 Ms letter, February 16, 1812, Ridgway Library.

7 Odell, *op. cit.*, II, 383.

8 *Aurora*, September 29, 1812.

9 See the files of the *Aurora*.

York, where it was made to arrive in the midst of rehearsal, in the presence of the actors, packed up exactly *like pieces we were in the habit of receiving from London. It was opened with great gravity, and announced without any author being alluded to.* None of the company were in the secret, as I well knew 'these actors cannot keep counsel, not even the prompter.'"[10] Although Wood then stated that when he made known the true author after six or seven nights the play "ceased to attract," his own account book of receipts, as Professor Quinn has shown,[11] contradicts him, as does Durang's remark that "it lost none of its interest after the mask was removed."[12] It had six other presentations between January 2, and February 15, 1813,[13] when "it was received with great approbation." During one of these performances General Barker at the fourth scene of the fourth act when a parallel between the situation in Scotland and that then existing between Great Britain and the United States is drawn, rose from his seat in a box and raising his cane cried "No, sir, no; we'll nail them to the mast and sink with the stars and stripes before we yield" which was followed by a patriotic demonstration on the part of the rest of the audience in which "the applause continued for upward of ten minutes and some time was consumed before the dialogue of the scene could go on."[14]

Marmion was put on again the next season, first being performed December 10, 1813, and repeated December 24th.[15] The 6th of January, 1814, the Philadelphia *Aurora* printed the following notice: "The managers of the New Theatre have determined to compliment the author of Marmion with a benefit; un-

10 W. B. Wood, *Personal Recollections of the Stage,* p. 188.

11 A. H. Quinn, *History of the American Drama from the Beginning of the Civil War,* p. 141, and *Diary and Daily Account Book of W. B. Wood,* ms University of Pennsylvania Library, Season of 1812–1813.

12 Durang, *op. cit.,* chap. li.

13 See files of the *Democratic Press* for those months.

14 Durang, *op. cit.,* chap. li.

15 *Aurora* for those dates.

known to the author and in his absence. There are few who need be informed that the author here alluded to, is a young gentleman of this city, Captain James N. Barker, of the 2d. regiment of the U. S. Artillery—a gentleman whose unassuming merit, and suavity of manners have endeared him to his acquaintances; and whose taste and talents are an honor to our city.

"This piece, the result of many months labor, previously to his entering the army, has been received with reiterated applause by many crowded houses, both in this city and New York. It is unnecessary to speak of the merits of the play, or to say anything on the encouragement due to the literary productions of our countrymen. The piece, with all its arrangements, is well known to the public. The managers of the theatre also, cannot pass unnoticed. Their conduct in getting up the piece unsolicited by his friends, at this particular time when the author is absent with his regiment on the lines, is highly honorable to them."

The 10th of January was chosen for the benefit and announced with this somewhat embroidered observation—"The representation of this piece naturally excites in the bosom of the spectators a lively interest for the author, who leaving the hills of Parnassus and the flowery vales of the Muses, to which he had both claims and attachments, has at the first call of his country devoted his talents, life and prospects in her cause—and the tended field so beautifully displayed, recalls vividly to our imagination, the author now surrounded with the same scenery in its rudest and roughest colors, that of reality.

"The patriotism of our city, it is hoped, will be displayed in the theatre, this evening, by a crowded house."[16] There was a storm that night and the receipts of $575.50,[17] not being "as extensive as the liberal wishes of the managers anticipated,"[18]

16 *Aurora,* January 10, 1814.

17 Wood's *Diary,* Season of 1813–1814.

18 *Democratic Press,* February 3, 1814.

February 7 was set aside for a second benefit, which was postponed until the next evening for the purpose of taking advantage of the presence of Commodore Perry,[19] who attended the performance that night. This combined attraction brought more satisfactory returns as Wood's *Diary* records the figures of $948.25, which in view of Barker's usual shortage in funds must have, in spite of the necessary help of the Commodore, been very acceptable.

Marmion was revived at the Anthony Street Theatre in New York, May 26, 1815.[20] May 20 and 22, 1818, it was given at the Olympic Theatre, Philadelphia, with a display of horsemanship as one of its features.[21] When Cooper came to the city in November, 1819, he appeared twice in the play "now altered and adapted to presentation."[22] James Wallack played it January 26, 1820, "with improvements"[23] that were undoubtedly the same alterations mentioned in Cooper's appearance. Barker's position as mayor of the city at the period was, unquestionably, a factor in these reproductions. The actress, Mrs. Burke, used *Marmion* "not acted these 5 years"[24] in her benefit, April 18, 1825, hoping, perhaps, to profit by the popularity Barker's *Superstition* had recently enjoyed, as did Duff for his benefit the same season "with the aid of forty horses."[25] Two more performances were given the next year, one on January 17, "the last time this season"[26] and another March 28 "by particular desire."[27] It was advertised at the Arch Street Theatre, January 4, 1834, with J. R. Scott in the part of Marmion,[28] and

19 *Ibid.*, February 7, 1814.

20 Odell, *op. cit.*, p. 439.

21 *Democratic Press.*

22 *Ibid.*, November 18, 1819, and Wood's *Diary* Season of 1819.

23 *Ibid.*, January 26, 1820.

24 *Ibid.*

25 Durang, *op. cit.*, chap. xxx.

26 *Democratic Press.*

27 *Ibid.*, March 28, 1826.

28 *Daily Pennsylvanian*, Philadelphia.

once more presented " in all its original splendor " by John Green, a Philadelphia actor, who March 29, 1837, offered for his benefit a " sumptuous bill of fare " that was to appeal to Philadelphians by its inclusion of " An American Play, by a native of Philadelphia. An American Farce, by a citizen of Philadelphia. The American Beneficiary, a native of Philadelphia." [29] What seems to be the last performance of *Marmion* took place February 28, 1848, at the new Bowery Theatre in New York,[30] appropriately enough the city in which it first reached the stage.

Barker wrote his own account of the sources of *Marmion*, indicating, of course, Scott's poem as the main one. In the second place, however, he went behind that for several personages and facts " for it was perceived, and not without surprise, that the cause of Scotland, '*His own, his native land*,' had occasionally found less support in the fine poetry of her gifted son, than from the simple relation, in homely prose, of the Suthron Hollingshead." [31] Further, in commenting on the American dramatization of Scott's poem *Rokeby*, in the third of a series of dramatic criticisms,[32] Barker just as definitely conveys his ideas on the matter of adaptation. " The writer of a drama drawn from a poem such as Rokeby," he declares, " is very apt to be either obscure or dull. His memory being warm with the subject in its whole scope and in all its particulars, he forgets that his audience may be less intimately acquainted with it; and, in selecting his materials, seizes therefore only the prominent incidents, without attending to the more removed points, which, nevertheless, may be altogether necessary to the coherence or elucidation of the story. But, in avoiding this, he sometimes falls into an opposite fault and either from deficiency of skill or want of inclination to prune and condense; or from an honest desire to leave nothing unexplained; joined perhaps to the pride of shewing how much

29 *Ibid.*, March 27, 1837.

30 J. N. Ireland, *Records of the New York Stage,* II, p. 455.

31 *Marmion,* 1816 ed., preface.

32 Pp. 66–67.

of his materials he can adapt to his purposes—overloads and impedes the action of his play, with barren occurrence and dry, uninteresting narrative."[33] Barker's own success in using these sources and in applying these ideas, without mere paraphrasing of Scott or obscurity and dullness of plot, explains the popularity of *Marmion.*

The opening scene of the play is that of Marmion's farewell to Constance. It creates a dramatic situation from a suggestion of Scott's in Canto III, part XV, and places emphasis upon their love story, which becomes a strand in the development of the tragedy. The scene is almost entirely Barker's, and is made effective by the striking verse and the frenzied appeals of Constance to the dead love of Marmion that Barker himself created. He then turned to Canto II and, for the second scene, introduced the visit of Clara and the nuns to St. Cuthberts. In these adaptations, as well as in others throughout the play, Barker at no time is a mere imitator. He skillfully reorders, condenses, or expands the episodes to his dramatic purpose and to the needs of lucidity and interest. He, too, contributes much of his own, especially by way of beauty of verse, motivation of character, and dramatic situation.

For the second act he uses the scene of the Scottish Hostel of Canto III, for his first scene, but centers the interest of the act upon Marmion's contest with the apparition in the person of De Wilton in the second scene, following parts XIX–XXI of Canto IV. Act III, after a first scene in an apartment in Whitly Abbey, which is not in Scott, and which is used to develop Clara's attitude toward Marmion, is concerned mainly with the dramatic trial, defence and sentencing of Constance in the Vault of Penitence. The stage setting here follows Scott's description in Canto II, parts XVIII–XIX, fairly closely; and Constance's passionate, defiant defence, while not verbatim, is within the general pattern of the poem. The elimination of characters, how-

[33] *Democratic Press,* December 16, 1816.

ever, and the increased compactness give Barker's version greater tensity of feeling and a noticeably stronger close.

The Scottish camp and the reception of Marmion as English embassador that inaugurates Act IV, the most forceful act of the whole play, incorporates material from Canto IV of Scott, parts VI–VIII and XXV–XXXII, and from Canto V, parts I–IV, that is pruned and shaped to the point of originality. The second scene, a street in Edinburgh, originates in Canto V, part VI, and while Douglas is one of Scott's characters, suggestions were taken from Holinshed [34] for his part in this as well as the incidents concerning him with King James in Scene 4. For the third scene Barker leaves Scott and in " an antichamber in Holyrood palace " introduces Lady Heron, mistress of the King, and turns for additional material upon her role to the chronicler, Robert Lindesay.[35] The closing scene of this fourth act is that of the royal court and, as Professor Quinn has pointed out,[36] Barker here reaches the greatest heights in *Marmion*. Canto V, parts VIII–XXIII, is partial basis for scene and situation. Holinshed was also drawn upon for aid in characterization; and, while there is no direct following, the correspondence there printed [37] between James IV and Henry VIII was used in part for James' spirited defiance of England. This dialogue, not in Scott, as explained by Barker in his preface,[38] parallels the affairs between the United States and England just previous to the outbreak of the War of 1812 when *Marmion* was written. The coincidence colors and explains the emotional nature of the speech while the quick perception by the audience at the Chestnut Street Theatre of the application of the following lines to con-

34 Holinshed's *Chronicles of England, Scotland and Ireland,* V, 478–479.

35 *History of Scotland,* pp. 176–177.

36 *History of the American Drama, from the Beginning to the Civil War,* p. 142.

37 Holinshed, *op. cit.,* V, 473–476.

38 *Marmion,* 1816 ed., p. v.

temporary events easily accounts for the patriotic demonstration that occurred there:

> *James:* My lord, the first base step
> Is ne'er the last! the foot that fear but moves,
> Fear still impels. Do you not ask us here
> To throw our armour off, and cower at home,
> Patient, till England find a time to treat?
>
> *Marmion:* Till Henry come from France.
>
> *James:* Why went he thither
> But to wage unjust war?
>
> *Marmion:* Your highness' pardon,
> He went to quell the general enemy,
> Of you, and all.
>
> *James:* The general enemy!
> Spare me, my lord, the stale, distasteful tale,
> I know it all. The nation the most selfish,
> Presuming, arrogant, of all this globe,
> Professes but to fight for others' rights,
> While she alone infringes every right.
>
> *Marmion:* I knew before your majesty was partial
> To those you most mistakenly conceive
> To be your friends and allies.
>
> *James:* Soul of Bruce!
> Were they not then our allies, when your king
> Sought to enslave us? who of all the world
> Came at our need, but they? by heaven, lord Marmion,
> England insults us with the trite complaint
> That we are partial, for she shows by this,
> She thinks our senses are too dull and blunt
> To know who wounds us and who gives the balm.
> But let that rest; my country's bloody page
> I will not quote. Its former friend and foe
> Be now forgot; we urge our present griefs.

Marmion: All that you can with justice, ask of England,
Henry will grant. But he requires your pause
Till he return from waging foreign war.

James: Yes: till, like Edward the flushed conquerer come,
To bid our blazing cities warm our hurts
To fresher anguish. 'Twas for this, my lord,
When on the border our commission met,
Each day blushed on some new and poor evasion
Of your commissioners—who strove at last
To cloak their shame in rude display of passion,
As cowards hide their fears with blustering.

Marmion: The subject may have been most intricate,
Your claims involved in doubt.

James: Not so—not so—
Simple as truth they were, clear as the sun.
But what did England during this our parley?
While thus negotiating, what did England?
When, trusting in your faith, resentment slept,
And patience stayed your tardy reparation
Of wrongs so long inflicted? It was then—
Even in days of truce! I burn to speak it—
Murder and pillage, England's constant agents,
Roamed through our land and harboured in our bays!
Our peaceful border sacked, our vessels plundered,
Our abused liegemen robbed, enslaved, and slaughtered.
My lord, my lord, under such injuries,
How shall a free and gallant nation act?
Still lay its sovereignty at England's feet—
Still basely ask a boon from England's bounty
Still vainly hope redress from England's justice?
No! by our martyred fathers' memories,
The land may sink—but, like a glorious wreck,
'Twill keep its colours flying to the last.

The fifth and last act opens with a scene in Douglas' castle where Marmion is guest at the King's command. Part XXXIV of Canto V furnished the germ of the idea, but the development is Barker's. The next two scenes, wherein Clara and De Wilton meet in an armoury of the castle and Marmion takes his belligerent farewell in the courtyard, are in substance from Canto VI, parts V, X–XVII of Scott's poem but in detail of action, dialogue and verse of Barker's invention. Surrey's pavilion in the English camp, scene 4, selects some of its subject matter from part XXIV, Canto VI, such as Marmion's arrival from Scotland and the battle plans of the English. The treachery of Lady Heron in her betrayal of James' secrets to Surrey seems to be a return to Lindesay's narrative,[39] but again a good deal more artful than mere imitation. The final action of the battle at Flodden, involving the actual contest, Marmion's death in the presence of Clara, and the reunion of Clara and De Wilton, has three sources—Canto VI, parts III, XXIV, XXVII–XXXII of Scott; the description of the fight in Holinshed;[40] and Barker's own imagination and experience in warfare.

The interruption of the War of 1812 prevented immediate printing of the play. It was, ultimately published by Longworth, New York, in 1816 and reprinted "very much curtailed"[41] in Lopez and Wemyss in their *Acting American Theatre*, Philadelphia, 1826, Barker evidently having no part in this edition, as it was taken from the prompt books and is without the author's preface of the earlier printing.

In his preface to the first edition Barker defined his attitude concerning American literature with unmistakable clarity. He deplored the lack of encouragement to write drama in America, a condition brought about not from fair criticism but "from a superciliousness, that freezes, from a neglect that destroys." He arraigned the contempt we, as a nation, had for ourselves, which in spite of geographic and political independence created a point

39 P. 177.

40 Holinshed, *op. cit.*, V, 480–482.

41 Dunlap, *op. cit.*, p. 379.

of view in which " a provincial sense of the inferiority still lingers among some, even of our highest minded, with regard to the arts and refinements of society." He flatly indicted the habit of looking to Europe for standards in taste—the fact that " we meanly condescend to learn from British reviews, British newspapers and what is still more contemptible, from romances of British travellers through our country, how to estimate the benefits we enjoy, and indeed, what to think of ourselves." He, in short, declares a literary and intellectual independence that should cause those in America, whose opinions are laws, to rise from a debasement and imitation that makes them " mental colonists of England." Further, to support and give reason to this independence, we in America should " acquire and maintain a steady, temperate, and consistent consciousness of our country's worth and value, without resorting to French naturalists to learn the size of our persons; or to British tourists to ascertain the state of our morals or manners; and, above all, without going, with superstitious reverence, a pilgrimage across the Atlantic to have our books stamped as orthodox by the literary pontiffs of London or Edinburgh." These convictions led Barker, in his turn, to do what he could to give American drama national independence. With " no very regular apprenticeship to the muses " he was nevertheless eager to do his share—" lowly commencements in making plays, as in manufacturing cloths, seem to be forced upon us by the fear of failure of those who have much to lose." The beginner in native playwriting should be encouraged so as to entice the best of American minds to engage in the enterprise—" or importation will have to continue from England." Barker's leadership in the making of native plays was not accidental.

In the meanwhile, however, Barker's interests were largely military. The first official step was his appointment by Secretary of War, William Eustis, as captain in the Second Regiment of Pennsylvania Artillery, May 26, 1812,[42] with orders to proceed to Carlisle, Pennsylvania, where General Bloomfield was in command. Barker's duties brought him back to Philadelphia in time to participate in a celebration of the 4th of July, when he was one of the presiding officers and read the Declaration of Independence [43] to a company of officers of the U. S. Army. He had apparently been assigned to the work of recruiting an artillery company in Philadelphia. He succeeded in rapidly organizing and training a unit of 106 men—upon whose departure for the Canadian front the Philadelphia *Aurora* of September 5, 1812, remarks, "Passed through this city on Thursday morning last, from their encampment on the west side of the Schuylkill, on their march to join their fellow soldiers at Albany, the Company of Artillery under the command of Captain James N. Barker. We were highly gratified at the order maintained by and the martial appearance of the men commanded by this brave young officer, and sincerely wish them that success which the glorious cause in which they are engaged so deservedly merits."

Later the same month Barker was in active service at the front. He volunteered to accompany Lieutenant Isaac Roach in an endeavor to steal two English vessels riding under the guns of Fort Erie. "Towson and Barker were so determined on going," Roach wrote,[44] "I began to think our tea party would be broken up, as Col. Scott and Lt. Elliott both declared no one should go to rank me." Barker lost the chance to go. In further elaboration upon his fellow officers Roach declares "I sincerely think there could not be a nobler collection of warm hearts and willing hands than the officers of the 2d Artillery then at head-quarters . . . not one individual of whom but is born on the reports as having been distinguished."

42 *Journal of the Executive Proceedings of the Senate,* II (1805–1815), 270.

43 *Aurora,* July 7, 1812.

44 "Journal of Major Isaac Roach 1812–1824," *Pennsylvania Magazine of History and Biography,* XVII, 131–143.

In December of 1812 Barker was in winter quarters with the army at Buffalo. The monotony of the routine and discomfort of winter encampment was now and again relieved by skirmishes and artillery exchanges with the enemy. In one such instance, when the British opened fire on a small boat plying along the American side of the river to show their guns were unspiked or replaced, the fire was quickly returned by the U. S. batteries and a smart cannonading continued for several hours—" during which the dexterity of our artillerists was evinced, in sending two 25 lb. balls from Captain Barker's battery, through the embrasure of a British redoubt; one of which dismounted their gun, and drove most of the men out of the battery. From the battery S of the last, being farthest up the river, our artillerists drove about 28 cannon shot through the buildings within Fort Erie, and another knocked open a gate in the wall. All we want in every department is practice." [45]

Shortly after this Barker returned to Philadelphia on recruiting service which was interrupted by his being placed in command of Fort Mifflin, on the Delaware, early in the spring of 1813, when the British invaded the Chesapeake and threatened the city. The regular U. S. troops had been withdrawn and the fort, consequently, was nearly defenseless. To fill the lack the " Democratic Association of Young Men " organized a " Junior Artillerists' Company " of about eighty officers and men, who, together with Captain William Mitchell's volunteer company known as the " Independent Blues," were sent down to Fort Mifflin on March 23, 1813, to do garrison duty under the command of Barker, assisted by Captain Williams of the Second Regiment of U. S. Artillery. These companies remained in the fort, being meanwhile thoroughly drilled and trained by Barker, until April 7, 1813, when they were honorably discharged and

[45] *Aurora,* December 29, 1812, letter quoted from Buffalo, dated December 6, 1812.

their places filled by U. S. troops.[46] General Bloomfield, who was in command of the military district, on the volunteers' withdrawal from Fort Mifflin publicly thanked captains Barker and Williams " for their unwearied diligence in the exercise and improvement of the militia in garrison duty." [47]

Returning, then, to recruiting duty Barker raised a second company of artillerists numbering 116 men. These were trained in Philadelphia during the summer and, according to the following extract from a New York letter, were early in September, 1813, on their way to the Canadian Border. " A few days ago we were highly gratified with the sight of Captain James N. Barker's company of artillerists, composed of 116 able bodied, soldierly looking men, on their way to Sackett's Harbour; the sight was truly a pleasing one to our citizens, who generally declared them to be the best company that had passed this place since the commencement of the war: and what added more to the general sentiment in favor of that meritorious officer was, that last year he had raised and led to Buffalo a company of 106 men, from whence he was shortly after sent back on recruiting service. Such zeal and activity in the cause of his country merit the approbation of all good men." [48] He evidently was on the Canadian Front until the spring of 1814, when, May 12, he was officially transferred to the Corps of Artillery with the rank of captain.[49] In the meantime, it would seem, he fought a duel with Major Wade Hampton, father of the Confederate general, in which encounter he was shot through both thighs and for several years incapacitated from active service.[50] Before the

46 See the files of the *Aurora* and Scharf and Westcott, *History of Philadelphia,* I, 563.

47 R. P. McCulloh, *Military Operations on the Delaware During the Late War,* pp. 4–5.

48 *Aurora,* September 16, 1813.

49 Files, War Department, Adjutant General's Office.

50 Henry Simpson, *Lives of Eminent Philadelphians Now Deceased,* pp. 25–29—also ms biographical sketch by a granddaughter, Mrs. Story, Keys Collection.

regular appointment as captain in the Corps of Artillery came through on May 12, he was, undoubtedly because of his incapacitation, made Assistant Adjutant General of the 4th Military District " with the brevet rank of Major "[51] by President Madison on April 8, 1814. This brought him back to Philadelphia which was then the headquarters of the 4th Military District.

During the fall of 1814, Barker was at Marcus Hook, where for a time the headquarters was located in proximity to the camp of the Pennsylvania troops. The newspapers for the period contain many orders and instructions issued from the Adjutant General's office over Barker's signature.[52] His duties were less dangerous but just as exacting of his time and movements as active service. With the breaking of the Marcus Hook camp, early in December, 1814,[53] the headquarters returned to Philadelphia. Barker remained as Assistant Adjutant General, until, under the provisions of the act of Congress approved March 3, 1815, reducing the army to a peace establishment, he was honorably discharged, June 15, 1815.[54]

Barker immediately re-entered politics, resumed his former connections with the party organizations in the city, and was given the Democratic nomination for the Pennsylvania Assembly on September 13, 1815.[55] The war reaction had set in, the election was bitterly contested; and, although Barker ran considerably ahead of his ticket, he went down to defeat with the rest of the party.[56] With the political squabbling that followed, politics must have appeared rather unpromising as a field for success or service. Barker turned again to the army and on May 17, 1816 was reinstated as Major and made Acting Assistant Adjutant

51 Official Commission, Keys Collection.

52 See files of the *Democratic Press* and *Aurora.*

53 *Democratic Press,* December 5, 1814.

54 Files, War Department, Adjutant General's Office, Washington, D. C.

55 *Democratic Press,* September 13, 1815.

56 *Ibid.,* October 12, 1815.

General of the U. S. Army, holding that rank and position until his resignation April 1, 1817.[57]

Sometime during the period of his war service, Barker saved the life of William Tyler, brother to President John Tyler, an act that later was a marked determinant in his career as a government official in Washington.[58] He, in addition, retained for years the friendships and contacts that came through service in the war. All through his later life he kept alive and active a strong interest in the affairs of the veterans of the War of 1812, aided in forming an officer's unit in Washington, and was in turn supported by them in his activities in the Treasury Department in a later era.

57 Files, War Department, Adjutant General's Office.
58 Washington *Globe,* February 14, 1842.

V

CRITIC, BIOGRAPHER, AND ALDERMAN

PREVIOUS to Barker's final withdrawal from the army in 1817, he had again taken up his literary interests. The appearance in June, 1816, of the following appreciation may have stimulated him to further writing—"Mr. Barker of Philadelphia, who should be emphatically styled the *American Dramatist*, has written a number of plays, that ought to be numbered among the standing stock of the theatre. He wrote a few years ago a play entitled Marmion, the plot of which is taken from Scott's Marmion. Barker's Marmion is decidedly more interesting that Mr. Scott's . . . and should be read by every man who is a lover of the drama and disposed to foster American genius. . . . Let it not be believed that in speaking thus of Mr. Barker's literary merits, I am actuated by friendship, or undue partiality for American productions. The fact is, I never saw that gentleman in my life."[1] The drama *How to Try a Lover* was in all probability begun shortly after this, although it didn't appear for a number of months; nor could *The Armourer's Escape* have been far behind in commencement, even though a good deal of non-dramatic writing intervened before either of them was given to the public.

The first products of Barker's post-war composition were two songs sung by him at the Democratic Celebrations of the 4th of July held at Spring Garden.[2] The first is on his favorite theme combining freedom, loyalty and democracy and was called "The Exile's Welcome." It strikes a serious note with the martial spirit of recent battle echoing in it and is carried at a somewhat lofty but stirring level. The second song is in sharp contrast

1 *Democratic Press,* June 25, 1816—quoted from the *New York Courier.*

2 *Democratic Press,* July 10, 1816, reprints these in its account of the event.

in mood and must have been markedly effective in its succession on the first. It is vivacious with a dashing, gay quality returning to the tone of *Tears and Smiles.* "The Day" is its title and that idea is used as a constant pivot for the turns of thought, playing about the custom of toasting the day. It follows in part:

THE DAY

Since a toast you demand, and I can't say you nay,
  I must task my invention to bring one;
But feeling quite sure that I've nothing to *say,*
  By your leave, I'll endeavor to *sing* one.
    But fill, while you may,
  That's the right way,
Or the *night* will be here, ere we drink down the *day.*

I'd give you The Day, but you've had it before;
  So *some other day* I must try, Sir;
From our Enemy's back I must borrow a *score*
  That we marked since the Fourth of July, sir,
    Fill while ye may, &c.

Then here's *to the days,* were they foggy or fine,
  That blushed on our foes early follies;
The day that the Yankees *Cornwallised* Burgoyne
  And the day they *Burgoyned* poor Cornwallis.
    Fill while ye may, &c.

And here's *to the days,* which, in fort or in plain,
  Lately shone on our rivals disasters;
And to all the *bright days,* that on Lake and on main,
  Saw his Fleets and his Frigates change masters.
    Fill while ye may, &c.

Barker, according to family tradition, was in much demand as a singer and drew great enjoyment from music whether his or another's. His singing was the butt of good natured satire in a periodical by the name of *Trangram, or Fashionable Trifler* in which he appears as " Billy Mushroom " several times, as, for instance, " Passing through the supper room, I stopped to hear Mushroom, the poet, who had proved himself less of a beau than a bon vivant: he was roaring out a song with good emphasis and discretion, and had left the company of the enchantresses to offer plentiful libations to the jolly God. From a circulating report, that Billy had lately been receiving instructions for the guitar and singing a l'Italiene, and from his having been taught to believe that he could, by satire or sympathy of his execution, produce either tears or smiles, I expected, that his affectation might have urged him to expose his insufficiency."[3] Simultaneously with these two songs a third one of earlier make, " Columbia Land of Liberty," was having a popular reception at Vauxhall Gardens as sung nightly by McFarland.[4]

Barker's literary production took to new channels on December 18, 1816, with the inauguration of an extended series of contributions of dramatic criticism to the *Democratic Press* of Philadelphia, for which he used his middle initial as signature.[5] He begins, in the first of his eleven installments, with a resumé of dramatic history and a defense of the importance and influence of the drama and the stage. This summary is authoritatively supported by concise quotation and accurate reference only possible from a wide, extended reading in history and dramatic literature. The defense develops from the statement that " Considered either as a school of Ethics, or as a source of a rational and refined amusement, the Drama has always claimed the protection of the enlightened and the polished classes of society." From Shakespeare's day it has been the mirror of the times. " It is true the theatre has sometimes suffered debasement from scenes unworthy of it; but it has never been totally without its redeeming merits. Even during the reign of debauchery

3 I, 1809, No. 1, 13.

4 *Aurora,* advertisements.

5 Ms letter by Editor John Binns, December, 1816, Ridgway Library, established Barker's authorship.

and wit, under Charles II, it did no more than reflect the manners of the court: the example of that execrable Monarch sanctioned every vice and the stage did but catch the fashionable infection." Opinions of eminent people and of the sternest moralists "might be adduced in support of the theatre, were it possible to suspect that any intelligent person on a candid view of the subject, could doubt the uniform and powerful tendency of a well regulated stage, to polish and improve manners, to chastise and correct vice, and to promote in various ways the best interests of mankind." As mere entertainment no other source is comparable in rational gratification and unwearying variety. The public indifference toward the theatre is deplorable in view of all which is there offered. "A neglect so strange would be unaccountable were it not that we can attribute it to—fashion—caprice—magical words, sufficient to account for any thing. Fashion that can give her routes on play nights, in order, most generously, to keep the theatre empty. Caprice that can leave Shakespeare, to run after the 'Hunted Taylor'"—which leads to a diplomatic but none the less devastating discussion of the circus with the opinion that "Abandoning the theatre for this species of entertainment, seems as if the student should quit the histories of Greece and Rome and apply himself closely to *Mother Goose*, or *Mother Bunch*." Barker's contention for the encouragement of native playwrights, his conviction of the worth of native plays, and his patriotism find expression in the wish that "it might be hoped that a higher destiny still awaits the stage than it has yet attained—that with a free people and under the liberal care of a government such as ours it might tend to keep alive the spirit of freedom; and to unite conflicting parties in a common love of liberty and devotedness to country."

"The Drama—No. II"[6] opens with the topic, "Taste of the Town"—which taste Barker finds to be promising if still somewhat meagre in quantity. Good taste is, to his satisfaction,

[6] *Democratic Press,* December 20, 1816.

found not only among the fashionable but in " those respectable citizens who equally removed from the high vulgar and the low, form in every society so numerous and independent a class, and on whose patronage public exhibitions must always mainly rely." The criticism of and running comment upon contemporary productions is then taken up. This embraces observation of acting, stage business, morals, and an unusual proportion, for that day, of genuine critical analysis. " Belle's Stratagem," as an instance of the latter trait, " possesses none of those gaudy adornments which we have been told are indispensable in order to attract at the present day. It is nothing more than a *good comedy,* formed on the genuine old model, but without its offensive indecency; and never degenerating into the wide-mouthed farce—or rising, if rising it can be called, into the mawkish sentimentality of more recent productions. Its plot is without labored intricacy, its incidents are natural, its characters such as are to be found among human beings; and its dialogue such as people of this world might be supposed to hold with each other. The approbation it excited from all parts of the house assured us that we can still even more than tolerate a play that has neither dogs, monkies, or horses to recommend it." An energetic justification of the theatrical managers against unwarranted complaints embodies an intimate knowledge equally of the gallery and the green room.

In the third contribution [7] Barker divides his attention between a new American play entitled *Rokeby* and a reply that had in the meanwhile been made [8] to his judgments upon the circus. The *Rokeby* matter is a keen, detailed dissection that has been touched upon elsewhere [9] and centered in the general statement that " After a patient attention to the performance of this piece, we are forced to give it as our opinion, that if it should add any-

[7] *Ibid.,* December 26, 1816.

[8] *Ibid.,* December 20, 1816.

[9] See pp. 50–51, discussion of *Marmion.*

thing to the character of our country in dramatic literature, it will not be by its representation on the stage in its present form." The rejoinder to the criticism on Barker's opinions of the circus is a suave, well bolstered answer filled with supporting historical facts and in its polite ease pointedly contrasts with the somewhat heated accusations of "unjust and illiberal" [10] that weave through these charges.

This controversy is soon quietly dropped by Barker although he persists calmly enough in other articles in the series to maintain his ideas. Installments four [11] and five [12] touch such matters as "A Word on Lovers' Quarrels," "Steele and Addison on Rope Dancers and Tumblers," "The Circus" and estimates of current plays, as *The Woodman's Hut, Wild Oats, Alladdin; or, The Wonderful Lamp* and others. The sixth contribution [13] starts with a synopsis of M. G. Lewis' *Bombastes Furioso* and after remarks on this, carries over to "Hints to Actors in Burlesque" the gist of the advice being a reminder that "Everything in burlesque is to be somewhat extravagant; but if too much heightened we lose its proper and delicate humor, and get in exchange nothing but rude open farce. A caricature should never be made so monstrous as to be deprived of all likeness." The next two numbers of *The Drama*, VII [14] and VIII,[15] continue to lay stress on acting in topics such as "Of the Different Styles of Acting in Tragedy," "Mr. Cooper in Hamlet and Macbeth," and "Richard III." Barker's constant theatre-going, his fine memory, his accurate and minute observation, and his personal experience in play-writing and production, give these opinions of his great practical worth.

Cooper's performance of the play, *Bertram*, gave rise to some

10 *Democratic Press*, December 20, 1816.
11 *Ibid.*, December 30, 1816.
12 *Ibid.*, January 6, 1817.
13 *Ibid.*, January 13, 1817.
14 *Ibid.*, January 22, 1817.
15 *Ibid.*, January 27, 1817.

opinions on dramatic poetry, as applied to that drama, which have interest in connection with Barker's own work. "Classical poetry," he stated,[16] "has become so bad of late years; and Gothic poetry so fashionable; and a modern tragedy with any kind of poetry at all, so rare a production; that perhaps we might venture to call *Bertram* a good play, if not positively, at least by comparison. Indeed, notwithstanding its wildness and improbabilities; the uncouth quaintness of some of its terms, and the *Southeyean* feebleness of some of its lines; it possesses many eminent beauties. And even the heaviness which an over portion of *monkery*, and too much mere poetry give some parts of it, is amply compensated for, by the boldness of its plan and incidents; the grandeur and strength of its principal characters; and the frequent vigor of its thoughts and language." Discussions of *Othello*, *Alexander the Great*, *Julius Caesar*, *The Castle Spectre*, and *The Wheel of Fortune* are the pith of the subject matter in the last two contributions, X [17] and XI,[18] which end with a section captioned "Farewell to Mr. Cooper."

This period in Barker's life indicates what he might have done if he had permanently given his undivided attention to literature. At this time his military duties had become nominal and he was for about the only time in his career enabled to devote himself largely to his writing.

Early in January of 1817 he was engaged in adapting or altering plays for W. B. Wood, manager of the Chestnut Street Theatre, who wrote to Barker that month "I send you two new Tragedies to read. *Fazio* appears to me to overflow with wild beauty. Is it not possible to shape it so as to enable me to act it? You did not return me the little drama since you altered it." [19] What "the little drama" was is unknown. Whether *Fazio; or, The Italian Wife*, one of Milmans' pieces, was

16 *Ibid.*, "Drama—No. IX," February 3, 1817.

17 *Ibid.*, February 14, 1817.

18 *Ibid.*, February 19, 1817.

19 Ms letter, January, 1817, Ridgway Library.

"shaped" for Wood or not is also obscure. According to Wood's *Diary* he put *Fazio* on twice in January and February 1819 [20] with no hint as to any adaptation.

How to Try a Lover must have been well along in the making at the beginning of 1817 since so early as January 11 it was advertised as in preparation in the theatre.[21] This notice was printed daily until February 6, when the play was then noted as in rehearsal and so advertised until March 4, when the notice was again changed to "in preparation" [22] and Barker's *Armourer's Escape* also began to appear as preparing in the theatre. They were so announced together until *How to Try a Lover* was dropped out, March 18, 1817, without explanation. Barker himself declared he did not know why *How to Try a Lover* was not acted and added "It is the only drama I have written with which I was satisfied." [23] It was suggested by *LaFolie Espagnole*,[24] a French novel with a Spanish story, by Pigault-Lebrun. It is more mature than *Tears and Smiles* but animated with a similar gay insouciance. It is one of the earliest treatments in American drama of the Spanish themes that became so popular with the playwrights in subsequent years as instanced, among others, by Robert Montgomery Bird's *The Broker of Bogota.*

How to Try a Lover is in three acts and seven scenes, laid in thirteenth century Spanish Catalonia. The action is concerned with the love of Carlos and Eugenia and the plans of their respective fathers, Counts Arandez and Almeyda, to join the two families as a seal to their life long friendship by the marriage of their children. Carlos, however, antagonized by threats of a year's confinement before his marriage in punishment for his youthful sins and the refusal of his father to reveal the name of

20 Philadelphia season, 1818–1819.

21 *Aurora,* January 11, 1817.

22 *Ibid.,* files for appropriate dates.

23 Dunlap, *op. cit.,* p. 380.

24 Paris, 1812–1814, 3d ed., 4 vols.

his intended lady, has adopted love and liberty as his motto and become a lover errant. He, in keeping with his usual habit, has fallen in love at first sight with the unknown Eugenia in a convent at Barcelona, but has been deflected in this pursuit by a mysterious beauty, set as a decoy by Almeyda on the principle that a man can be led where he can't be driven, who has lured him half over Spain and into difficulties with the local authorities of a village in the neighborhood of Count Almeyda's castle. Rescued by the unknown troops of the Count, he has been left with his valet, Pacomo, in a wood near the Count's castle where the opening scene of the comedy takes place. The fathers, in the belief that pretended mystery and difficulties will but add to the ardor of the lovers, scheme to furnish them with both. Carlos with the aid of Pacomo, a genuinely humorous character, makes his way into the castle. Count Almeyda opposes his desire to see Eugenia and informs him that she is already promised in marriage. Spurred by that news, Carlos and Pacomo, the latter in love with Eugenia's maid Flora, break into the castle vaults that same night after having informed Eugenia of their intentions. After some first rate comedy in which Carlos, Pacomo, Flora, and Beatrice, an amusing, shrewish spinster in Count Almeyda's service, play the main roles, Carlos makes his way to Eugenia where he is found by Counts Almeyda and Arandez, seized, and held for trial the following day by a medieval Court of Love. Eugenia, according to the laws of chivalry, presides at the court. Beatrice is made prosecutor. Count Almeyda acts as Carlos' advocate. Through the agency of Flora, Eugenia in the meanwhile has discovered the scheme of Count Arandez and her father and through her presidency of the court takes vengeance upon them by pretending to condemn Carlos in a vivacious, clever scene sparkling with delightful dialogue that closes with the awarding of her hand to her lover and the revelation of her knowledge of the purposes of the fathers.

The plot was chosen almost entirely from the incidents of the fourth volume of *La Folie Espanole*, Barker disregarding the salacious adventuring in the first three volumes and eliminating similar material of the fourth volume. He condensed the time element to twenty-four hours, brought the incidents into more unified relations to one another, emphasized those that threw the love story of Carlos and Eugenia into relief, and created a coherent, compact drama from the incidental, rambling narrative of this picaresque novel, testifying in this to his genuine dramatic skill. The episodes selected are little changed in the majority of cases and even in several places, such as the first entrance into the castle, the later descent into the vaults, and the scene of the Court of Love are fairly accurate translations of the French original. The stage setting given for the exterior of the castle and the hall of the Court of Love together with the descriptions of costumes are, also, only slightly altered. The characters themselves have been renamed with the exceptions of the servants, Pedrillo and Gusman. The name Pacomo, in the original, that of a minor character, was transferred in the comedy to the delightful squire of Carlos, known as Trufaldin in Lebrun's story. Carlos, named Mendace in the French source, Pacomo, Flora, and the two counts have been pruned and disinfected morally with the result of making them more normal, believable people. Pacomo particularly, shorn of his rascality, becomes an admirable creation. The dialogue has been considerably expedited in *How to Try a Lover* and possesses an ease and gayety that render it one of the impressive traits of the play. This is in sharp contrast to the somewhat lumbering conversation in the novel. Barker, however, has retained the telling portions of Lebrun's dialogue and skillfully blended the translation with his own contributions into a harmonious whole. The closing scene of the Court of Love in the third act draws its pointed effectiveness largely from the art of this blending. The play is a well knit, ably constructed one, with marked dramatic characteristics originating in Barker's own gifts.

How to Try a Lover was produced the first time, nineteen years after its composition, for Burton's benefit on March 26, 1836, under the title *The Court of Love* taken from the scene in the play similarly named, which Barker thought to be a striking stage novelty when he first wrote the comedy. It ought to be explained that his letter to Dunlap,[25] in which he said the play was not acted, was written four years before the production occurred. The cast on the opening night included Kline as Count Almeyda, Faulkner as Count Arandez, Wood as Don Carlos, Burton as Pacomo, Miss Emma Wheatly as Donna Eugenia, Mrs. Thayer as Flora, and Mrs. Jones as Beatrice.[26] The press comment was limited to the Democratic paper, *The Daily Pennsylvanian,*[27] which reads "The comedy of 'The Court of Love,' by J. N. Barker, Esq. performed for the first time on Saturday evening, at the Arch St. Theatre, for Burton's benefit, went off with much spirit and effect, and was warmly applauded. It is a lively, agreeable piece, and notwithstanding the disadvantage of a first representation, hurriedly got up, made a highly favorable impression. The performers, particularly Burton, Wood, and Miss Wheatly, did ample justice to their respective parts, and drew down frequent and hearty approbation. The comedy is one that will bear frequent repetition"—all of which must easily have been true, judging from the play, as its humor is of the first order and its structure most skillfully built. It was repeated April 27, by the same cast with the exception of Miss Wheatly whose part of Donna Eugenia was taken by Miss Pelham, and again on May 14 of the same spring.[28]

In 1817 there was some comment and interest in a story known as *A Narrative of the Adventures and Sufferings of John R. Jewett.*[29] Jewett himself was the author and had published this

25 Dunlap, *op. cit.,* pp. 376–380.

26 *Daily Pennsylvanian,* March 26, 1836.

27 March 29, 1836.

28 *Daily Pennsylvanian.*

29 *Analectic Magazine,* Philadelphia, 1817, IX, 141.

relation, " of a Captivity of nearly three years among Savages of Nootka Sound: With an account of the Manners, Mode of Living, and Religious Opinions of the Natives," in New York the year before. He had been the armourer and only survivor of the ship *Boston* and rather mistakenly seized on this means of earning some money. The book didn't sell; and it was, in all likelihood, in a further effort to capitalize these experiences that Jewett prevailed on Barker to dramatize the story for him. This was done in the opening months of 1817. There was a good deal of feeling on the question with England over the settlement of the Oregon dispute and some enthusiasm, naturally, for any one who had had part in an adventure connected with that country. "The only copy of the piece was taken by Jewett," [30] to quote Barker, and was permanently lost sight of. The scenes and characters, though, have been preserved in Durang,[31] the theatrical advertisements [32] and a play bill.[33] The play was called *The Armourer's Escape; or, Three Years at Nootka Sound.* It was composed of two acts of five and two scenes respectively, was dubbed an " historical melodrama," " attempted an accurate sketch," and, as staged, aimed " to represent faithfully the costumes, manners, ceremonies and superstitions of these extraordinary people, by as rigid an adherence to the narrative as the stage will permit." Jewett himself took the part of the armourer; Robertson and Jackson were chief officers of the ship Boston; Thompson, Jewett's companion in adventure by Mr. Jefferson; Maquina, Nootkian king, Barrett; Nachee Utilla, king of the Klizzards, Mr. T. Jefferson; and others, with Mrs. Jefferson and Mrs. Harris as Indian princesses. The sequence of scenes not only traces the story, but also indicates adornments and extras. Sc. 1, Maquina destroys the crew of the Boston—

30 Dunlap, *op. cit.,* p. 380.

31 First Series, chap. liv.

32 *Democratic Press,* March 20, 1817.

33 Collection of play bills, Historical Society of Pennsylvania.

except Jewett and Thompson. Sc. 2, Village—Jewett's artifice to preserve Thompson's life succeeds. Sc. 3, Wood—remainder of the crew who had landed for provisions, surprised and slaughtered. Sc. 4, interior of Maquina's house—Chiefs and women—An attempt at accurate representation of funeral ceremonies over the body of a chief. Sc. 5, Village of Nootka—Moon eclipse—Ships discovered on fire at a distance—Nootkians attacked by the Aycharts, a neighboring tribe who are discovered and defeated—their mode of approach accurately represented. Act II, Sc. 1, Nootkians dressed in the habits of the murdered crew—a procession of the more civilized Klizzards whose chief, Utilla, enabled Jewett to get word to his deliverers—Ludicrous ceremonies of the Bear—Nootkian war dance—Jewett sings the Nootka war song—He is forced to select a wife and chooses Princess Yuqua—Dance of Nootkian girls. Chiefs enter to carry them off, masked with heads of animals—Girls rescued and a general dance follows. Sc. 2, Shore—American brig at a little distance—Maquina seized by the captain as a hostage for Jewett and Thompson, who are released and Maquina restored—Song of the Armourer's Boy by Jewett at the end of the melodrama.

The play had received preliminary notice as early as March 14, 1817,[34] and was first presented at the Chestnut Street Theatre, March 21,[35] repeated March 22, and given as Jewett's benefit March 24,[36] which he doubtless deserved.

It was this year, also, that Barker's earlier interest in sketching some of the national figures of the period materialized. In 1816 the first part of the first volume of Joseph Delaplaine's ambitious *Repository of the Lives and Portraits of Distinguished American Characters* was published with unsatisfactory reception by the public. A rather surprising controversy arose over

34 *Aurora.*

35 *Democratic Press,* March 21, 1817.

36 Woods' *Diary,* season of 1816–1817.

its merits that swelled in volume and bitterness in the magazines [37] and newspapers,[38] involved the President of Princeton and reached so far as Thomas Jefferson in retirement at Monticello. In his quite human desire to adjust matters Delaplaine secured Barker as the author for the six biographies that were to make up the second part of the first volume. While the biographies were anonymous, Delaplaine's choice of Barker, especially in the light of the dispute, would indicate that Barker's reputation as a man of letters was well recognized and established. It was announced that "he has secured the best aid and profited by the criticism." [39] To take on the authorship of a work that already had created vigorous enmity was risking failure, but was exactly the kind of thing that had an attraction for Barker's active, adventurous spirit.

At any rate, Delaplaine was clamoring for the manuscripts by the middle of June, 1817, and appealed to Barker to expedite matters. He supplied Barker with some of the material for the lives and finally writes on July 17, 1817:

"Tomorrow I shall send you something respecting Gov. Clinton—and in a day or two perhaps, something of Jay—after this I don't expect to receive anything more of any persons whose lives are in hands—

"The printer disliked to begin the half vol. till the manuscript of it is finished. May I then request the favour of you to have the goodness to complete the whole as soon as possible. The delay of publication has induced many in different parts of the United States to believe that the work has been abandoned. Independent of this, the suspension of publication causes me to lose at least ten dollars daily." [40]

This last letter had been preceded by one the day before which closed

[37] *Analectic Magazine,* VIII (1816), 193.

[38] *Democratic Press,* November 5, 1816; January 29, February 17, 1817.

[39] *Ibid.,* July 16, 1817.

[40] Ms letter by Joseph Delaplaine, June 17, 1817, Ridgway Library.

"I beg you, dear sir, to have the goodness to close your manuscripts." [41]

This second part of the *Repository* included characterizations of Peyton Randolph, Thomas Jefferson, John Jay, Rufus King, DeWitt Clinton, and Robert Fulton. They are not unrivalled in excellence but are as good as any of the period. They are of the older form of laudatory biographical composition with their subjects upon the pedestals that public opinion had already begun to erect for them. The style is high running and rhetorical with a stiff formality. DeWitt Clinton, for example, had not only an imposing array of virtues, gifts and excellencies, but "As a writer, his style is neither gorgeous nor unadorned. Not destitute of the beauties of language and embellishments of fancy, nor simply stale or insipidly tame and cold, it preserves a medium between the rugged and the weak, the inflated and the low, and is adapted with a happy and natural skill to the very numerous and dissimilar topics which, from time to time, it embraces. Didactic, serious, and impressive, when the subject requires; learned and scientific when necessary; gay and sportive when proper; his pen displays a versatility of power which few men possess. . . . His range of information and acquaintance extends from all that can interest to whatever may divert and gratify." [42] Barker's patriotism stresses what in these men is characteristically American. It is his loyalty that withholds any of the flaws or weaknesses in these native leaders that would make them less perfect but more human.

In spite of the pressure and hurry, the acceptance of this second half volume of the *Repository* was more satisfactory. The *Democratic Press* had "a conviction that the style, research and impartiality of the writer of the lives will command very

[41] Ms letter by Joseph Delaplaine, June 16, 1817, Historical Society of Pennsylvania.

[42] *Repository,* I, Part A, 189.

general approbation." [43] It was praised for neatness of style, correctness, and good judgment, while one writer in the *New York Evening Post* goes so far as to call the author of the *Repository* "The American Plutarch." [44]

In anticipation, apparently, of procuring a commission as alderman in the place of his father, Barker resigned from the U. S. Army on April 1, 1817.[45] His duties by that time were routine and sterile and a future military life in peace time must have offered a dull prospect. He accepted Governor Simon Snyder's appointment to the office of alderman, April 2, 1817,[46] and from this date to his death was active as a political official and more intimately than ever involved in political movements and the affairs of the Democratic party. In keeping with this new stimulus to his political interests he delivered the main oration at the 4th of July celebration of the "New School" of Democracy [47] held at Vauxhall Gardens. This was somewhat slashing in its eloquence—"for my theme is the happiness, the glory, the independence of my country." He touched upon freedom in South America, the influence of the Declaration of Independence, Congress, American statesmen and warriors, and dramatically eulogized the part that Philadelphians took in securing independence—many of whom, including his father, were in the audience. With his military experiences so close behind him he became satirical on peace societies. "But such societies most generally grow out of the rankest hypocricy, or the grossest ignorance. How weak! as if folding your arms would prevent the blow from reaching you. How preposterous! as if the phenomena of the moral, were not as natural as those of the physical world. War as necessarily proceeds from the

43 *Democratic Press,* July 16, 1817.

44 *Ibid.,* December 31, 1817, quotes the whole criticism.

45 Files, War Department, Adjutant General's Office.

46 Official Commission, April 2, 1817, Keys Collection, and *Democratic Press,* April 8, 1817.

47 *Ibid.,* July 7, 1817, printed it in full.

conflicting passions of man, as the thunder storm issues from the elements." Preparation and precaution will prevent war, he quite modernly declared. He assailed Federalism as synonymous with the worst aristocracy even though " There are, in this party, many good and sensible men, but how they came there it would be difficult for me to guess, and, probably, impossible for them to tell." He concluded in the vein of " our government and our people." It is first rate oratorical writing and was well summed up by one of the toasts following its delivery, on " The Orator of the Day—His Sentiments are those of a Soldier, a Patriot, and a Citizen." [48] Good though it must have been in effect Barker must have read with mixed feelings a statement in the *Democratic Press* of July 10 that " In this consummate Phillippic, no small share of the keen, nervous, concise sublimity of Demosthenes, and the majestic melodious flow of Cicero are united." The oration was, at the request of the meeting, immediately printed in pamphlet form,[49] widely quoted by both the new and the old school Democrats and used not only by them but by the Federalists as political ammunition.

The failing health and subsequent death of General Barker, April 3, 1818, engaged Barker's attention during the spring of that year. He took out papers of administration for his father's estate on June 10,[50] and was busied in private affairs in that connection for some weeks. He read the Declaration of Independence at the Court House on July 4th and by that date seems to have fully resumed his political interests.

His unflagging enthusiasm for the drama and the theatre found still another medium for outlet through his becoming one of the stockholders of the Olympic (Walnut Street) Theatre in

48 *Ibid.,* July 7, 1817.

49 Collection of pamphlets, Mercantile Library, Philadelphia.

50 Office of the Register of Wills, Philadelphia, Adm. No. 144, 1818–Bk. M, p. 96.

October of the same year.[51] This kept him in close touch with the inner circle of theatrical affairs and gave free access to the theatre at any performance. The playwright and critic had now also become alderman and patron.

[51] *Olympic Theatre, Proceedings and Resolutions,* Philadelphia, 1819, p. 21.

VI

THE MAYORALTY AND AUTHORSHIP OF *SUPERSTITION*

OWING, it would seem, to the precedent of his father as well as to his own aggressive energy, Barker announced his candidacy for the office of sheriff of Philadelphia, July 1, 1819.[1] He was, among more than a dozen others, an active contestant for the nomination until the end of July when a temporary peace was patched up among the party factions in order to present an unbroken front in the fall elections; and Barker, to aid in establishing the desired harmony, withdrew his name. The Democratic victory in October resulted in that party's control of the Philadelphia councils and on October 19, 1819, Barker was chosen from among the aldermen, who only were eligible, as mayor of the city.[2] He seems to have been regarded as a compromise candidate who would distribute the positions at his disposal in accordance with factional voting power. The efficiency of his appointments, consequently, aroused considerable animosity and some of the ward organizations passed resolutions censuring him for selecting men who were not, in their minds, the right kind of Democrats and declaring intentions to refuse to support him on any future occasions. There was some disorder in these meetings; while, at the same time, other wards gave him unstinted support.[3] Retrenchment had been one of the campaign slogans, and on the day of Barker's election the matter of reducing the major's salary from $3,000 to $2,000 a year was taken up by the councils.[4] He was an honest politician and a fearless one.

1 *Democratic Press,* Files for July and August show the political developments.

2 *Poulson's Advertiser,* October 20, 1819.

3 *Democratic Press,* January 12, 27, 1820.

4 *Ibid.,* October 19, 1819.

Barker's concern in the problem of slavery was in harmony with his steady support of freedom and justice. Few men have been more consistent in life long support of principles than he. Accordingly, when a town meeting on the subject was held on November 23, 1819, he seized the opportunity to bring both his official and personal support to the aid of the cause.[5] He took part in drawing up a memorial to Congress petitioning that body to prohibit slavery in any new state.

Always a philanthropist, he used his office for altruistic purposes whenever need arose. When news came of the suffering and destitution caused by the burning of Wilmington, S. C., he called a town meeting to consider sending aid and became himself chairman of a committee to raise money for that purpose[6] in December of 1819. The 27th of the following month, he was secretary of another meeting held at the city hall to organize relief for the victims of the Savannah fire that had nearly wiped out the town earlier in January.[7] He, William Tilghman and others, also petitioned the Pennsylvania Assembly to coöperate, which resulted in a vote to donate $15,000 to be sent to Savannah by Governor Findley.[8]

Barker's term of office was not without adventurous activities. From early February on through the spring of 1820 there was a wave of robberies and numerous attempts were made to fire the city, causing a reign of dread and terror. By February 23, 1820, the nightly watch was doubled and the mayor announced through the press that he would accept volunteers for nightly patrols whose expenses would be borne by the city.[9] The situation grew steadily more alarming and in March was further complicated by a well organized revolt of the prisoners in the city jail which necessitated the mayor and sheriff calling upon Gen-

5 *Ibid.*, November 25, 1819.

6 *Ibid.*, December 21, 1819.

7 Sharf and Westcott, *History of Philadelphia.*

8 Ms letter, January 31, 1820, Ridgway Library.

9 *Democratic Press,* February 23, 1820.

eral Cadwalader for aid in quelling an uprising which for a time seemed likely to grow out of all control.[10] Finding still additional steps necessary as further safeguard against the thieves and incendiaries, Barker addressed a message to councils April 6, 1820,[11] in which he asked for additional police and funds to enable him to secure the extra services of public officials and set a reward of $1,000 for the detection of any incendiary. The next day, by public proclamation,[12] he assured the citizens that all was being done to remedy affairs and urged them to help the watch and volunteer patrols in every possible way. They were urged to inspect their houses carefully before retiring and to overlook the annoyances the patrols may have caused through the necessity of all citizens answering the official challenge.

Barker's military experience came in good stead in his organizing of the city forces. The following letter to city councils sufficiently elucidates his efficient methods of using the police and citizens. It is representative, too, of the adequacy of his style in official documents and correspondence:

To the Select and Common Councils

Gentlemen—

I have the honor to state for the information of councils, that in conformity with their resolution of the 6th ins. I have with the aid of the City Commissioners organized an additional nightly watch or guard. In order to carry the view of councils fully into effect, under the extraordinary circumstances that existed, I have thought it expedient to divide the city into five districts, each district to be placed under charge of an officer with a competent force; his guard-house for obvious reasons to be near as possible in the centre of his district. The whole number of privates embodied is 186, all of whom together with their officers are on duty every night, from early in the evening, until daylight the next morning. The compensation

10 *Aurora,* March 19, 1820.

11 Ms message in letter form, April 6, 1820, Historical Society of Pennsylvania.

12 *Democratic Press,* April 8, 1820.

of the officers has been fixed at $35 and that of the men at $20 each per month. These sums together with contingent expenses, will amount to $2,000 per month. The volunteer Patrols had been allowed under the provision of the ordinance of Dec. 14th, 1816, a reasonable sum for the reimbursement of their actual necessary expences, the aggregate sum to be paid them, will it is presumed, at least equal that to be paid to the present guard. Every praise is unquestionably due the citizens for their services so promptly rendered in the emergency, but it is conceived, from the selection made in forming the present guard, from the subordination and the nature of the duties to which they are subject, from the plan of their organization and the character of their officers, that they will prove the more efficient safe-guards. I have the gratification to add that since they have been placed on duty the streets have been kept thoroughly clear of loiterers, vagabonds, and suspicious persons; and that occurrences calculated to produce alarm have sensibly diminished if not wholly ceased.

I have also appointed under the authority of the resolution, already adverted to, three police officers, and have fixed their compensation at $48 33/100 each per month. Although I myself am fully of opinion, that the expenses consequent on these arrangements, were necessarily called for by the occasion, I have deemed it proper to submit this statement to councils, as early as possible, in order that their wisdom may decide upon the expediency of their continuance.

I have the honor to be
Yr. most Obt. Sevt.
JAMES N. BARKER

Philadelphia, April 26, 1820.[13]

These steps were efficacious and the mayor informed Councils June 8, that on the 3d of the previous month the city guard instituted for the protection of the citizens had been disbanded.[14]

Barker's handling of municipal finances was markedly suc-

[13] Ms letter, Historical Society of Pennsylvania.

[14] Ms letter to Councils, June 8, 1820, Historical Society of Pennsylvania.

cessful and stimulated an interest in the problems of general financing that later gave him a position as an authority on that subject. It gave him experience that afterward came to bear on his duties as Collector of the Port and First Comptroller of the U. S. Treasury. Four loans were satisfactorily arranged varying from $20,000 to $200,000 in amount,[15] and the routine financial matters conducted economically in line with promises of retrenchment. The fall elections of October, 1820, placed the Federalists in control of both branches of city councils, however, and when they met for the election of the mayor on the 17th of that month Robert Wharton was chosen to succeed Barker.[16] It was a purely partisan matter. The Democrats had once more split and the entire city ticket went down to defeat.

The increased prominence that the mayoralty had brought Barker required more pretentious living quarters. It involved him in numerous social and non-political matters of Philadelphia life. He as a result, moved his home from the northwest corner of Prune and Fourth Streets where he had been living for several years, to the north side of Chestnut Street above Eleventh,[17] a more pretentious if less interesting neighborhood. It was, of course, his own bookish interest and democratic leanings, not merely his influential prominence that led to his signing the constitution of the Apprentices' Library in February of 1820—the oldest free circulating library in America.[18] More largely on account of his position and growing name as a financial authority, but in view likewise of his enthusiasm for music, he was made a manager of the Musical Fund Society, May 3, 1820.[19]

15 *Democratic Press,* April 21, May 23, June 4, August 22, 1820.

16 *Poulson's Advertiser,* October 18, 1820.

17 Paxton's *Philadelphia Directory,* 1819, and McCarty and Davis, *Directory,* 1820.

18 J. F. Lewis, *History of the Apprentices' Library,* Philadelphia, 1924.

19 Ms letter of Secretary J. K. Kane, May 3, 1820, Ridgway Library.

The same month of the following year he was elected a director of the Pennsylvania Institute for the Deaf and Dumb.[20]

At the close of his term as mayor, Barker resumed his business as alderman at No. 16 S. 5th Street, 2d door above Chestnut [21] and continued active in the politics of the day. He was a member of several partisan committees and as such was a firm advocate of harmony within the ranks and continually struggled to unite discontented groups that sometimes turned on him with spiteful irritation.

Personal loss during these months must have made such matters weigh tiresomely upon his mind. Family ties with him had always been among the deep, true things he loved. The death of his daughter Mary, February 8, 1820, that of his son James, on New Year's day of the next year, followed by the fatal illness of the oldest boy, John, December 26, 1821 and of his small three-year-old daughter, Ellen, in the first week of 1822 [22] must have rendered the problems of local politics futile and the rhetoric of ward leaders empty gesture.

From the end of 1821, however, until his appointment to the collectorship of the port of Philadelphia by President Jackson, Barker as one of the recognized Democratic leaders of the city participated in practically all of the political developments of those years. He was chairman of Democratic town meetings, again active in ward organizations and on the 4th of July, 1824, delivered a keynote speech by way of the oration of the day that became the theme for much rabid political discussion and squabbling in the press. At the meeting of the Democratic General Ward Committee, held September 2, 1824, the members agreed upon Barker as their candidate for Congress. In an attempt to adjust more factional misunderstandings, his name was ultimately removed from the ticket, much to the surprise of the op-

20 *Democratic Press,* May 7, 1821.

21 *Ibid.,* advertisement, October 23, 1820.

22 Records of the Laurel Hill Cemetery Co. for lots 71 and 81, Philadelphia.

position papers which considered him the best man in the party to win the election. A Democratic Town Meeting was held in protest against Barker's withdrawal September 21, 1824, but adjourned because of disorder.[23] His friends and enemies were invariably wholehearted.

The preliminary work to animate Andrew Jackson's 1828 campaign for the Presidency included a public meeting held in Philadelphia, May 26, 1826[24] from which Barker emerged as one of the Committee of Superintendence to handle Jackson's affairs in the city. Although Barker's literary and cultural traits differentiated him from many of the followers of Jackson, his political creed, military training and aggressiveness created a sympathetic admiration for General Jackson which grew into a life-long loyalty to the personality and policies of that most picturesque of American Presidents. As a 4th of July oration, 1827, he delivered a Jacksonian eulogy stirring to a degree that caused some of the audience to beat a man who had drunk a toast to Mr. Clay, but the outburst was fortunately somewhat dampened in effect by a heavy thunderstorm which ended the demonstration before it developed disgraceful proportions.[25] The speech became campaign material and was, as a matter of fact, a reasoned analysis and sound appreciation of Jackson's position. As a member of the "Jackson Club"[26] of Philadelphia and as a delegate and Secretary to the Democratic convention at Harrisburg which nominated Jackson, he was given wide publicity as an ardent advocate of General Jackson.[27]

There were other public affairs of the period with which Barker was associated. In keeping with his high enthusiasm for freedom and its struggles, he was a leader and director of

23 See files of the *Democratic Press,* 1822–1824, for details of local politics.

24 *Ibid.,* May 26, 1826.

25 *Ibid.,* July 5, 1827.

26 *American Sentinel,* Philadelphia, June 12, 1828.

27 *National Gazette,* Philadelphia, January 11, 1828.

public sentiment in sympathy with the Grecian fight for freedom and in drawing up and transmitting a petition to Congress in December of 1823 [28] asking for the recognition of the independence of Greece. Part of his admiration for Lord Byron seems to be explained by that poet's connection with the Greek war for liberty. As the state legislature had in mind a move from Harrisburg in 1827, an agitation was begun in Philadelphia to bring the state capitol to that city. This appealed to Barker's community loyalty, as the Greek cause had to his love for democracy, and materialized in a town meeting with reference to the transfer.[29]

Of necessity Barker's literary activity was curtailed, though always active, during his mayoralty term and by the absorbing political affairs of the following few years. As a member of the Musical Fund Society he was called upon in 1821 to alter the words in the Alleluia of Beethoven from the Mount of Olives to make them more suitable to the purpose of a public concert.[30] The occasional production of *Marmion* must have continued his dramatic interests, while the fact that he took the trouble to secure a pass from W. B. Wood [31] and possessed one to the Olympic Theatre as a share holder would indicate a fairly steady attendance at the theatre.

His contact with the drama took more productive form in 1824, when his "serious dramatic tale," [32] *Superstition; or, The Fanatic Father*, was first played at the Chestnut Street Theatre, March 12.[33] According to the advertisement for its second performance, which took place on March 17, 1824,[34] it had been on

28 *Democratic Press,* December 13, 1823.
29 *Ibid.,* January 19, 1827.
30 Ms letter of Benjamin Carr, January 11, 1821, Ridgway Library.
31 Ms letter of W. B. Wood, November 22, 1821, Ridgway Library.
32 Dunlap, *op. cit.,* p. 380.
33 *Democratic Press,* March 12, 1824.
34 *Ibid.,* March 17, 1824.

the first night "received with the most flattering approbation." The playbill for the 17th lists the cast as follows: [35]

Sir Reginald Egerton	Mr. Warren
George Egerton	Wemyss
Ravensworth	Mr. Darley
Walford	Mr. Wheatly
Charles Fitzroy	Mr. Wood
The Unknown	Mr. Duff
Isabella, Charles' mother	Mrs. Wood
Mary Ravensworth	Mrs. Duff
Alice Walford	Mrs. Durang

Durang remarks that it "indeed, deserved the many able euloguims paid to its merits by our best dramatic critics. Yet this excellent production like all its American kind was suffered to pass into oblivion." [36] Mrs. Duff, as Mary, had a great success that enabled her to outshine Mrs. Wood as Isabella, a situation that Wemyss declared prevented Manager Wood from producing the play a greater number of times [37] and shows, as Professor Quinn writes, that "Truly, 'the manager's wife' has had a potent influence in the records of our stage." [38] In 1826 *Superstition* was published in *The Acting American Theatre* by Lopez and Wemyss.

The theme of the play is native, the scene a New England village about 1675. Through envy and superstition the villagers have come to look upon Charles Fitzroy and his mother, Isabella, with suspicion of evil and sorcery. They have lately come from England in search of Isabella's father. Ravensworth, the local minister, incensed by their disregard of his pious rule and the love of Charles for his daughter, Mary, fans the hate

35 Collection of play bills at the Historical Society of Pennsylvania.

36 Durang, *op. cit.*, chap. xviii.

37 C. F. Wemyss, *Twenty-six Years of the Life of an Actor and Manager,* I, 88.

38 A. H. Quinn, *History of the American Drama from the Beginning to the Civil War,* p. 147.

and leads the persecution. The basic motives of the drama are found in the conflict between this Puritan bigotry and the love of the two young people. Returning from college, Charles meets the Unknown, but is unaware of the fact that he is really Isabella's father and one of the judges of Charles I seeking secret asylum from the vengeance that Charles II meted out to the regicides. Contrasting humor is introduced through Sir Reginald Egerton and his nephew George, sent in search of the regicide by Charles II. Charles arrives in time to protect Mary from George's amorous advances, which results in a duel in which George is wounded. The village is then attacked by the Indians, and the inhabitants are on the brink of disaster, when the Unknown suddenly appears, rallies the villagers, with the aid of Charles and Walford, turns defeat to victory, and then just as suddenly disappears. This mysterious assistance and the fact that Charles is untouched although in the thick of the fight are used by Ravensworth to throw further suspicion on Isabella as a sorceress. Isabella persuades Charles to flee and in a forceful scene informs him of her purpose in America and of her secret marriage.

Isa.: Poor boy, poor boy! Well Charles, the time is come
And if my spirits fail not—you shall know all.
Your father—but I cannot, no, I cannot
Commence my story there.—I was left, Charles,
Without a parents' care, just at that age
That needs it most. I had ne'er known my mother,
And was scarce fifteen when my father's fate
Forc'd him to abandon child and home and country,
For he had been a patriot, as he deemed it,
Or, as his destiny decreed a traitor—
He fled to this new world.

Charles: Does he yet live?

Isa.: Alas! I know not, rumours came to England
That he survived. It was to find my father,

And on my knees implore his benediction;—
Haply, should he forgive, to minister
Unto his ages comfort—I came hither.

Charles: 'Tis strange, if living, he should seek concealment,
After the general amnesty.

Isa.: O! Charles;
He was excepted in that act of mercy:
He had done that, the king might never pardon.

Charles: Unhappy man!

Isa.: Most true.—But let me haste
To close my dark recital I was plac'd
In charge of a kinsman—a perfidious villain
Whose avarice sold, betray'd me—O my son,
It is not fit thy ears should hear the tale,
And from my lips. I wept, implor'd, resisted—
Riches and pleasure tempted me in vain
Coupled with shame. But hellish craft at length
Triumph'd o'er credulous variety—The altar
Was made the scene of sacrilegious mockery
The holy vestments of the priest, became
A profane masking habit—

They are summoned to trial. Charles goes to Mary to bid her good bye and a love scene of fine delicacy and touching beauty takes place. The climax of the play is reached when Charles is surprised by Ravensworth in the midst of his farewell to Mary, is accused of attempting her honor, seized and hurried to the scene of the trial, the time of which has been put forward, to join his mother already there.

The last scene is that of the trial in the village church, in which Ravensworth acts as prosecutor. The procedure is developed by Barker into a tense, tragic conclusion. Isabella's defence against superstition and cant forces Ravensworth to secure his vengeance by redirecting his charge, this time against Charles for the murder of George Egerton, attempted violation of Mary, and sorcery through the strange appearance of the Unknown. Charles, to protect Mary, refuses to plead, which in the old law meant death. Ravensworth, taking advantage of this, and through his power over the people, persuades them to summarily execute Charles.

Rave: Hear ye this Judges! People, hear ye this
(*Storm commences*)
And why do we delay! His doom were death,
Disdaining as he has to make his plea
To the charge of sorcery. Now, his full confession,
Which ye have heard, dooms him a second time.
(*Storm increases: Thunder and Lightning*)
Then why do ye delay? The angry Heavens—
Hark, how they chide in thunder. Mark their lightnings.
(*The storm rages; the* Judges *rise; all is confusion; the* People *and two* Officers *gather around* Charles; Officers *seize him.*)

Isab.: Save him! O Heaven! As ye are men have mercy!

Rave: No; not beneath this roof, among the tombs
Under the fury of the madden'd sky;
Fit time and place!

Charles: (*As they are dragging him out.*) Mary; my Mother!
Mary!

Isab.: My son!
(*Leans nearly fainting in* Lucy's *arms*)

Mary: (*Reviving*) Who calls me? Ah! What would ye do?
He's innocent—he's my betroth'd—my husband!
He came with my consent—he's innocent!

Rave: Listen not to her; 'tis his hellish magic
Speaks in her voice—away!

Mary: O Charles, my Charles!—(*She faints*)
(*They bear* Charles *out—The storm continues*)

Rave: It is accomplished.

Mary revives as Charles' body is brought back, begins to plead for him, sees what has occurred, loses her mind and dies. Sir Egerton appears, declares Charles recognized by the king as his son, and carries a pardon for the Unknown, who has arrived too late to aid his daughter, who dies in his arms.

The main events of *Superstition* were, as Barker wrote, "said to have actually occurred in New England, in the latter part of the 17th Century . . . found recorded in the authentic history of that dark period." [39] This authentic history was, without much doubt, Governor Thomas Hutchinson's *History of Massachusetts.*[40] In this are found not only material used in the general background, but also suggestions for characterizations and the ground-work for at least two main incidents of the play—the saving of the village by the regicide, Goffe, and the trial for sorcery that ends the tragedy. Barker handled this subject matter artfully. He moulded it to his dramatic needs. He rearranged events, supplied convincing motives for much of the action, filled out many of the characters, entirely created others, and shaped a definite inevitable plot.

Of the principal incidents derived from Governor Hutchinson, those concerning the regicide Goffe parallel the history most accurately. The relationships of "The Unknown" (Goffe), Isabella, and Charles were invented, but probably suggested by the Goldsmith letters in which Goffe and his wife secretly corresponded under the guise of mother and son, using the names Frances and Walter Goldsmith.[41] Goffe's secret cave at Hatchets' Harbor, near New Haven, used by him as a hiding place on several occasions in 1661 and 1664, was transferred to the neighborhood of Salem by Barker, the time post-dated eleven years, and the cave made the scene of Charles's visit to The Unknown in Sc. 1, Act II. The Indian attack on Hadley, Mass.,

39 *Superstition,* Preliminary explanatory note, Lopez and Wemyss ed.

40 2 vols., 3d ed., Boston, 1795.

41 Thomas Hutchinson, *The History of Massachusetts,* I, 200 N.

1675, the sudden appearance of Goffe, the rallying of the villagers to successful resistance, and his mysterious disappearance that left the people " in consternation, utterly unable to account for this strange phenomenon," [42] were in Act III, Sc. 2 worked into one of the most effective portions of the drama. Barker substituted Salem for Hadley, created the details of setting and action, heightened the supernatural effects and brought the bare incident to life. The contact of Goffe with witch trials was hinted in a statement from his diary, quoted by Hutchinson,[43] referring to three witches condemned at Hartford in 1662, and probably suggested the connection that Barker brought about in having Goffe appear in the sorcery trial that closes the play. Historical chronology was, of course, disregarded.

The characters of Ravensworth and his daughter Mary had their origin in those of Rev. Samuel Paris and his daughter of Salem village.[44] In 1692 Paris's niece and daughter, aged ten or eleven, were supposedly bewitched, and through their accusations inaugurated the Salem witchcraft craze in which Samuel Paris took an " over officious " [45] part, and which he directed with such insane harshness. In the play the situation is altered and dramatically intensified by the introduction of the love story of Charles and Mary, the creation of the character of Isabella, and the joint influence of these upon the minister. The role and motives of Mary, the daughter, are necessarily raised and strengthened in *Superstition*. Here unselfishness and high ideals take the place of the deceit and cruelty of Elizabeth Paris. The impressive force of Ravensworth's individuality is largely Barker's own. The Rev. Paris, with the exception of his cruel bigotry, is vague and flat in Hutchinson's account. It required genuine creative art to turn him into the dynamic, living Puritan of the play.

42 *Ibid.,* II, 23 N.
43 *Ibid.,* II, 23 N.
44 *Ibid.,* II, 29.
45 *Ibid.,* II, 31.

The trial of Giles Cory at Salem in September, 1692,[46] furnished some of the basis for the tragic trial scene in Act V. Cory, convinced of the unfairness of the procedure, refused to plead, and as a consequence of standing mute was pressed to death. While it is not clear that Charles was so executed in *Superstition*, he does lose his life primarily through his refusal to plead, and the Cory case is the only one so ending in New England records. Charles' motive, however, was the protection of Mary, while Cory's was based on property rights and protest. The law and procedure of the trial scene are quite realistic according, at least, to Governor Hutchinson's narrative. The hurried nature of the trial in Barker's work takes its source in the fact that the Salem trials were put forward several months in order to remove opportunity for change of opinions or measures, as well as for the reason that several women of the most reputable families were accused.[47] Aside from the general superstitious background and his tragic fate, Cory has contributed little to the character of Charles. It is true that he was regarded as a suspicious person in the neighborhood, as Charles was, but he was an old man who had lived in the community for years with none of the personal traits of Barker's hero. The working up of the threatening atmosphere of fear and dread in Ravensworth's speech in the culminating scene gathered some items from Hutchinson's discussion. The references to the appearance of a comet as an omen of great evil and to the frequent blighting of crops originated there.[48] The title and main theme of the play also, possibly, might be attributed to the sentence in Hutchinson's comment on the Cory trial that " In all ages of the world, superstitious credulity has produced greater cruelty than is practised among the Hottentots, or other nations, whose belief of a Deity is called in question." [49]

[46] *Ibid.,* II, 60.
[47] *Ibid.,* II, 61.
[48] *Ibid.,* I, 201 N, 207.
[49] *Ibid.,* II, 60.

It is an interesting matter of literary history that Cooper in 1829 used the regicide story in *The Wept of Wish-ton-Wish;* and that Hawthorne in 1833 made it the subject of *The Gray Champion.* The witchcraft mania was also later used by Longfellow in the second of his *New England Tragedies, Giles Cory of the Salem Farms,* in which he embodied the same historical trial that Barker had judged good material for literary treatment. The New York playwright, Cornelius Mathews, in *Witchcraft, or the Martyrs of Salem* of 1846 likewise used Salem witchcraft for his material. The general subject, in addition, of Colonial history connects *Superstition* with a group of plays of which it is the first and ablest. *William Penn* by R. P. Smith, *DeSota* of G. H. Miles, a second drama by Cornelius Mathews entitled *Jacob Leisler,* the joint work of John Kerr and Samuel Chapman named *Son and Father,* and Elizabeth O. Smith's *Old New York* are the most important in this relationship.

Superstition was revived by the Laboratory Players at Columbia University, March 5, 1927, with a success sufficient to justify its repetition by that group on April 21, 1928. The second performance was most efficiently directed, well acted and admirably staged and an altogether fair and complete test of Barker's dramatic art. The play acted even better than it reads. It came to life on the boards with real animation. It built up in genuine dramatic fashion gathering momentum in feeling and tragic tensity. The Indian attack on the village, Isabella's confession, the love scene in Mary's apartment, and the trial scene grew into one another and concentrated pointedly in the motives, emotions and inimitability of the closing deep tragedy, indicating that Barker was a true playmaker in situation and emotion. The trial and its use of traditionary law and mob feeling was impressive even in view of the final holocaust. Barker knew the theatre and its successful devices and the scenes just mentioned were most effective stage pictures. The motives of characterization, further, were lucid and logical on the stage.

The action and reaction of character on character were definitely materialized and the minister, Ravensworth, stood out as an unusual personality powerfully conceived. The asides of the various roles were handled with judgment and restraint admirable even today; while the humorous touches in George Egerton and his uncle went over with spirit. They were spontaneous and merry. The whole dialogue was surprisingly natural when placed in its proper setting and conditions, losing entirely the suggestion of stiltedness apparent in the mere reading of the piece. In fact, the drama carried along through the imaginative power of the lines themselves and depended in a comparatively small way on help from stage scenery and theatrical mechanism. The beauty of the blank verse in rhythm and meaning played an important part in the unmistakable success of the revival.

Even in view of Barker's own statement that *How to Try a Lover* was the only drama that he had ever written with which he was satisfied,[50] *Superstition* is without question the best of his plays. Its construction, poetry, and insight into character, motives and history are not merely mature but of an excellence that marks *Superstition* as the best American drama composed until that date. It is an appropriate climax to Barker's dramatic career.

Barker's patriotism and reverence for the fathers of the Revolution made the visit of General Lafayette to Philadelphia in 1824 a significant occasion. He was a contributor to and one of the managers of the civic ball given in honor of Lafayette at the Chestnut Street Theatre, September 4, 1824,[51] thought at the time to have been the most brilliant social public function in the city's history. When the General paid a second visit to Philadelphia some three weeks later, a monster parade and celebration were held on September 24. All the various trades were represented in the line of march, as well as all the military, civil

50 Dunlap, *op. cit.,* p. 380.

51 *Democratic Press,* September 4, 1824.

and religious groups. The printers of the town as the center of their section of the parade had a press at work, mounted on a wagon, that threw off to the crowds innumerable copies of an ode that Barker had composed for the event at their request. It was gotten up in the form of a broadside [52] with decorated margins to set it off, and was reprinted in full several days afterward in one of the newspapers.[53] The first three stanzas are devoted to the early history of Lafayette and thoughts on human greatness as preface to those on the immediate events. The veneration for Lafayette, the feeling of gratitude, the wide-reaching inclusion of a national welcome and the enthusiastic appreciation of Lafayette's service to the United States seem well suited to the occasion and hence effective occasional verse.

His Americanism found partial expression in an interest in the past and the pioneer spirits who founded the colonies and sketched the broad outlines for later building. It was this fondness for history that is the basis for another poem of merit in 1825 read before the Society for the Commemoration of the Landing of William Penn, of which he was a member. The anniversary was signalized by a dinner given at Masonic Hall at which President John Quincy Adams, the Duke of Saxe-Weimar, Edward Livingston, members of Congress and about seventy members of the society were present. This poem was, too, an ode, entitled *The Pilgrims of Pennsylvania.* It is typical of Barker's ease in meter and clarity of thought. He always had the facility, even to a too great degree perhaps, to convey the conventional and appropriate ideas. The closing verses of this poem are illustrative:

> But ne'er shall their mem'ry be lost in the land
> That their toils to their offspring bequeath'd,

[52] A copy is preserved in the manuscipt room of the Historical Society of Pennsylvania.

[53] *National Gazette,* Philadelphia, September 30, 1824.

And oft shall each name of the patriot band,
In praise and in blessing be breath'd.

And still shall be sacred the spot where it stood,
The Elm in its time-honour'd age,
When Penn won the land without battle or blood,
And the savage bowed down to the sage.

It was popular enough at the time to be printed in full in the *Democratic Press*[54] and seems to have contributed to Barker's local reputation as a poet. A similar anniversary was the inspiration for an undated ode simply labeled "Ode for the Commemoration of the Landing of Penn." This is printed as a broadside apparently for distribution among the audience.[55] It is made up of six ten-line stanzas with the last two lines in each instance summarizing the other eight. The final couplet of the concluding stanza bears the pith of the whole thought:

When else, and where else was the word ever spoken,
That never was sworn to, and never was broken.

The point of view of the Indians is here emphasized recalling *The Indian Princess* and vague hints as to Barker's having been an authority on Indian lore.

Among the Philadelphia group of playwrights in 1827 was Dr. James McHenry, an Irish physician and poet, a friend of Barker's through their common interest in the theatre. Barker was constantly at the disposal of his friends and readily gave what prestige was his by writing a prologue for McHenry's *The Usurper*, a romantic play on early Irish history,[56] put on December 26, 1827, at the Chestnut Street Theatre when the prologue was spoken by Wemyss[57] with "emphasis and propriety . . . and loudly applauded." The prologue was com-

[54] December 31, 1825.
[55] Keys Collection.
[56] *The Usurper,* Philadelphia, 1829.
[57] *Democratic Press,* December 26, 27, 1827.

posed in quick moving rhymed couplets "complimentary to the Emerald Isle,"[58] McHenry and the drama. This received a much more favorable reception than the play, was commented upon as the main feature of the production and published in the Philadelphia *National Gazette*[59] and *The Casket* for February of 1828. It touched also upon the drama in general "with energy of wisdom fraught" while the line "The drama scorned by bigot and by fool" drew some sharp discussion.[60]

Richard Penn Smith, another of the Philadelphia group, could have found no one more appropriate as an author of a prologue to a play on Andrew Jackson than his friend Barker. *The Eighth of January* actually was inspired by Jackson's election of 1828 rather than by the battle of New Orleans, and Barker had just been as active and energetic a supporter of Jackson as there was in the city. Wemyss again spoke the prologue on the opening night of January 8, 1829, at the Chestnut Street Theatre, and it was pronounced "far above anything which has appeared in the shape of theatrical addresses this season."[61] It is neat and apt throughout and good naturedly satirical. It characteristically advanced a claim for American plays on native themes.

> And critic fops may sneer, and stand aloof,
> Because the fabric's western, web and woof—
> Americans who would be truly free,
> Will never scorn *domestic industry,*
> Nor while each foreign frippery claims admission
> Deny their *homespun* chance of competition.[62]

Jackson appears as:

[58] *United States Gazette,* Philadelphia, January 1, 1828.
[59] January 3, 1828, tri-weekly edition.
[60] *Ibid.,* January 5, 1828.
[61] *American Sentinel,* Philadelphia, January 13, 1829.
[62] *Eighth of January,* Philadelphia, 1829.

54675

> . . . warrior, sage-stamp'd by the hand of fate,
> Alike in valour, wisdom, virtue—great!
> . . . .
> Who never yielded yet—the conqueror who
> Conquered the conquerors of Waterloo.

Politics, patriotism and playmaking are cleverly blended into an effective prologue for that particular play. Barker's ability at occasional verse, to which type this really belongs, was not only of an admirable quality, but unfalteringly responsive at any time he wished to apply it.

American sympathy for the valiant contest the Greek nation had waged for independence was once more surging upward in 1827, and Barker again came forward in its behalf. The situation in Greece, through starvation and disease, was believed desperate. Work for relief was rapidly organized and at a meeting early in January he became secretary for a Greek Fund and took charge of directing the charity in Pennsylvania.[63] The almost daily meetings of the committee, the necessity of urgent appeals through the press, the handling of funds and supplies, and the arrangements for foreign transportation, required much time and thought. A vessel was chartered to sail in March with 10,000 barrels of supplies,[64] and by the end of July two ships had been dispatched.[65] Gathering of funds went on all through the fall and winter until April, 1828, when the work was brought to completion and Barker, as secretary, published an address to the citizens of Pennsylvania giving an account of what had been done and expressing the gratitude of the committee for their response.[66]

A veneration for ancient Grecian glories through love of history had, with other factors, been back of Barker's work with the

63 *Democratic Press,* January 12, 1827.

64 *Ibid.,* February 22, 1827.

65 *Ibid.,* July 20, 1827.

66 *American Sentinel,* April 7, 1828.

Greek fund. It was the same love for the past that had caused him to join the Historical Society of Pennsylvania a year earlier. He became a member of a standing committee " On the principles to which the rapid population of Pennsylvania may be ascribed,"[67] and served on the Executive Council of the society from 1827 to 1829.[68] Richard Penn Smith, C. J. Ingersoll and David Paul Brown were other Philadelphia dramatists belonging to the society that made these literary figures in the city even more intimate in a common taste for history.

October 24, 1827, Barker became the historian in a lengthy address, before the Society for the Commemoration of the Landing of William Penn, on the subject of " Primitive Settlements on the River Delaware." At the request of the meeting this was published in pamphlet form with the addition of copious notes and references.[69] It was reprinted in *Hazard's Pennsylvania Register*[70] and reviewed favorably in the Philadelphia *Album*[71] and the *National Gazette*.[72] He began this speech with a discussion of the desire and worth of looking into the past and gave a defense of American traditions against the sarcasm of European historians—adding an appeal for the preservation of valuable historical matter while deploring the waste of invaluable material belonging to the past. A careful exposition of the first settlement on the Delaware, near Gloucester, followed. He recounted Indian history associated with the settlement period, discussed the authenticity of the traditions concerning Walter Raleigh, Lord Delaware and DeVries; painted an imaginatively vivid picture of infant Philadelphia, lauded Penn as one of the

67 Memoirs of the Historical Society of Pennsylvania, Philadelphia, 1826, I, Part 1, 11.

68 *Charter and By-Laws of the Historical Society of Pennsylvania,* Philadelphia, 1880.

69 J. N. Barker, *Sketches of the Primitive Settlements on the River Delaware,* Philadelphia, 1827.

70 I (March, 1828), Nos. 12 and 13.

71 February 27, 1828.

72 February 27, 1828.

mighty minds of history and ended with the following touch of the grand manner:

"While we gratefully acknowledge the Providence that conferred, and can, alone, continue the blessings we rejoice in, let us not forget those chosen instruments, the pilgrim patriarchs, who amidst the desert, laid the foundations broad and deep of that temple to civil and religious liberty, which, soon towering above the forests of the west, the nations beheld and hailed as their hope, and which future generations of freemen will make their mark and model." [73]

In the course of the pamphlet the correctness of some of the historical facts in Dr. James Mease's *Picture of Philadelphia* had been questioned. This provoked a reply from Dr. Mease in answer, also in pamphlet form, called *A Reply to the Criticisms by J. N. Barker on the Historical Facts in the Picture of Philadelphia.*[74] In this the author, in numerical detail attempted a refutation of Barker's references, in turn charged inaccuracy in the *Sketches of the Primitive Settlements on the River Delaware,* lost his temper completely, descended to personalities, and generally failed to shake the reliability of Barker's account. This attack received and needed no rejoinder.

The demands of public life and the responsibilities of new official duties in the spring of 1829 for a time made Barker primarily the man of affairs—incidentally the playwright, poet, and historian.

[73] P. 38.

[74] Philadelphia, 1828.

VII

COLLECTOR OF THE PORT, 1829–1838

BARKER'S vigorous participation in Andrew Jackson's campaign for the Presidency in 1828, his personal friendship for and general support of General Jackson in verse, orations, and toasts were recognized with an appointment as Collector of the Port of Philadelphia, March 11, 1829.[1] And while even as staunch an opposition paper as the *United States Gazette* believed "the public will be gratified by the appointment,"[2] Barker was harshly attacked by John Binns, editor of the *Democratic Press*, representing a faction of the party opposed to Jackson and augmented by disappointed office seekers. The immediate cause of the onslaughts was Barker's removal of Binns as Custom House printer on March 25, 1829.[3] The new Secretary of the Treasury, S. D. Ingham, had had a collector of his own selection in mind and in his disappointment at Barker's designation by the President raised difficulties over Barker's furnishing of the required bonding that seriously threatened his acceptance of office.[4] The spoils system made patronage and office-seeking veritable manias. Survival of the friendliest was the law.

Barker conducted the affairs of the Custom House most adequately with necessary attention, at the same time, to political expediency. The records of the Custodian of Records at the Custom House in Philadelphia covering Barker's regime show the most meticulous, painstaking procedure in all matters.[5] The appointments at his disposal were numerous with many applicants for each position. His difficulties as mayor with chagrined

1 *American Sentinel*, March 13, 1829.

2 March 13, 1829.

3 *American Sentinel*, March 25, 1829.

4 *Pennsylvania Inquirer*, Philadelphia, November 23, 1830.

5 An extended series of Letter Books, for the years 1829–1840, contains the originals and copies of a good proportion of the collector's correspondence comprising at least two thousand letters.

expectants made him move with much caution. His decisions were generally satisfactory, especially to Washington.[6] Family loyalty, political coloring and efficiency fortunately coincided in the granting of a commission as Inspector of Customs to Barker's brother-in-law, Edmund Rogers, whose art had proved unremunerative; and whose brother, Benjamin Rogers, likewise eligible, was appointed to his place at the former's death in 1833.[7]

The duties of the collector were exacting, varied, and somewhat surprising. They included supervision of all repairs in connection with the custom house, ranging from roof mending to the overhauling of harbor boats; and the details of the management of the Marine Hospital were in his care.[8] Now and again a more colorful matter would arise as that contained in a letter from Secretary Ingham on November 27, 1829, presenting information from the Department of State as to numerous articles recently stolen from the palace of the Prince of Orange. These, so suspected the minister of the king of the Netherlands, were being smuggled into the United States. The collector was to turn detective, and a list of seventy-six items was inclosed. This, among other objects, enumerated "a string of 58 large pearls," "a large diadem of brilliants," and, as the last, "several old portraits of the Grand Dukes Alexander Constantine, Nicholas, and Michael painted in their youth."[9] About half of the articles were discovered in New York the following July.[10] The routine duties as seizure suits, questions of tariff, immigration, and fraud investigations required voluminous correspondence with nearly all the executive officers of the government, including the President. Evidently all matters of alien ad-

6 *Letter Book, Correspondence with the Departments,* April 13, 1829.

7 *Ibid.,* October 14, 1833.

8 *Letter Book, Correspondence with the Departments,* 1829.

9 *Ibid.,* November 27.

10 *American Sentinel,* August 3, 1829.

mission were directly referred to him.[11] The collector, further, was responsible for government property in his district, including Fort Mifflin, which Barker had put in order and repaired.[12] Then the beginning of Jackson's warfare upon the United States Bank delegated to Barker, as collector, the unpleasant task of personally withdrawing the government bonds and deposits from Nicholas Biddle's institution and placing them in the Girard Bank,[13] the accomplishment of which drew to him personally some of the bitterness thus engendered. Subsequent to the second election of Jackson, Barker was re-commissioned collector on March 5, 1833.[14]

Ever thoughtful of those under him, Barker constantly endeavored to secure better pay, improved working conditions and more consideration from the Treasury Department for the clerks and minor officials at the Custom House. Sometimes this was attempted in individual cases, at other times for the group. Success was variable and always difficult.[15] This ingrained thoughtfulness for those dependent upon him accounts for a good deal in Barker's life of both failure and success.

From the beginning of his political life Barker had been a sort of occasional spokesman for the party in Philadelphia, his literary gifts being indispensable in matters of press publicity and campaigning. Consequently when Secretary Ingham was attacked by several Philadelphia editors in 1829 Barker was called upon for a biographical sketch of that official. This has not survived, but seems to have made the desired impression.[16] In 1836 he forwarded several orations to Levi Woodberry, then Secretary of the Treasury, whether for his use or approval is

11 *Letter Book, Seizures and Suits at Law,* 1831.

12 *Letter Book, Correspondence with the Departments,* 1832.

13 *Ibid.,* September 26, 1833.

14 *Ibid.,* March 5.

15 *Ibid.,* 1834.

16 Ms letter of George M. Dallas, Nov. 7, 1829, Historical Society of Pennsylvania.

obscure, but as there is no mention from either end of their return the former purpose is the likelier.[17] These things, also, were part of the duties, if unofficial, of a literary collector.

Just as in his advocacy of Jackson, so in Van Buren's case Barker was one of the first of his Philadelphia adherents. As early as 1828 he had named one of his sons Wade Van Buren in an analogous manner to the christening of a daughter Rachel Jackson. At the annual celebration of the 8th of January, 1834, he had toasted Van Buren to the effect that "There is no station too high for merit to attain by the suffrage of a free-people," [18] and, of course, threw his influence behind Van Buren in the campaign of 1836. Meanwhile there was much clamoring for Barker's post as collector. Its influence and $4,400 salary [19] loomed large in the eyes of starved politicians, several of whom were stimulated to a belief in the theory of "Rotation in Office" and began a movement to apply it on Jackson's retirement. Barker was condemned for not resigning his office.[20] Van Buren gave him a third tentative appointment "till the end of the next session of the Senate and no longer." [21] The limited nature of the commission was not made public, with the consequence that a more definitely organized effort was made against Barker. The Democratic County Convention drew up resolutions of advice to Van Buren,[22] and the Democratic General Ward Committee followed their example.[23] If Barker was perturbed, not the slightest trace of his agitation showed itself.

The financial panic of 1837 caused him a good deal more irritation than had the officer seekers. The government issued orders for the collection of all revenue in specie.[24] The collector

17 *Letter Book, Correspondence with the Departments,* March 16, 1836.

18 *Daily Pennsylvanian,* January 11, 1834.

19 Register of the United States Government, 1837.

20 *Daily Pennsylvanian,* files for January and February, 1837.

21 Official Commission, Keys Collection.

22 *Daily Pennsylvanian,* April 6, 1837.

23 *Ibid.,* April 17, 1837.

24 *Ibid.,* May 16, 1837.

was to retain the gold in his own possession if there was any likelihood of the bank he customarily used suspending payments. The personal retention of large amounts of gold was rather dangerous and increased the shortage. The inability to pay in specie held up great quantities of goods at the Custom House and was bitterly resented, Barker unavoidably sharing in the blame.

Finally, February 23, 1838, Van Buren nominated Barker First Comptroller of the United States Treasury, the appointment to be effective March 1. His friend, James Buchanan, then a Senator, had apparently manipulated the whole affair, and informed Barker the same day of the Senate's approval.[25] He was to succeed George Wolf, former governor of Pennsylvania, who was given the collectorship Barker was vacating. A good deal of satire followed in the opposition papers on this exchange of positions and quite some speculation as to Barker's relinquishing a $4,400 post for an office paying only $3,500.[26] The comptrollership was, however, in official ranking, a promotion. The men in the Custom House had become attached to him through long service and his soliciting of the Treasury Department on their behalf and presented him with a large pair of specially designed silver cups expressive of their attachment for him.[27]

Barker, it would seem, was not unwilling to go to Washington. The bitterness of partisan squabbling and ruthless office grabbing had alienated a number of his friends and given rise to personal criticism of the sort least easily forgotten. Philadelphia had become uncomfortable. Most important, however, was the death of Mrs. Barker on October 31, 1837.[28] Added to the profound individual loss was the responsibility of five children, and the breakup of his domestic life. It was the uprooting of at-

25 Ms letter of James Buchanan, February 23, 1838, Keys Collection.

26 See files *United States Gazette* for March, 1838.

27 *Daily Pennsylvanian,* March 30, 1838.

28 *Ibid.,* November 1, 1837.

tachments to which he had given the best of himself and marks the turn of his career. Philadelphia had become painful as well as uncomfortable. Waning interests brought flagging energy. The aggressive belligerency so typical of the man became less fiery.

While Barker's position as federal office holder prohibited direct participation in local politics such as his customary chairmanships, ward committee work and election activity; he had a hand, nevertheless, during these years in many occurrences of a political cast. Public functions were rather regularly aided and attended. As guardian of administration policies in Philadelphia, he became involved in a dispute in the pages of the *American Sentinel* over an insult to President Jackson during May of 1831. His opponent was a Colonel S. B. Davis, who wrote over the signature of "a Democrat." It all had its origin in the President's antipathy for the United States Bank and a misapprehension that slurred the state legislature. Barker wrote as "A Subscriber" although both men's real names were at once divulged. "Mr. Barker," so Davis wrote at one stage in the exchange, "I am told, is a Poet, and this may account for some of the flights of fancy in which he indulged." [29] Barker, after replying bluntly to some other of Davis' points touches this one. "For the rest, 'A Subscriber,' may have a taste for 'flights of fancy' in their proper place, as the Gallant Colonel himself no doubt also has; but both the Gallant Colonel and 'A Subscriber' prefer, it is to be hoped, plain truth in political prose, which is the very reason that 'A Subscriber,' disliked the ambiguity on which he took the liberty to make a few remarks: for although employed in the public service, as the Colonel observes, 'A Subscriber' thinks he may innocently occupy a leisure moment, so far to follow the habit of many years, as to write an occasional article for the public papers, when he thinks it may be service-

[29] May 28, 1831.

able to the cause he espouses." [30] This dispute led to a good deal of uproar and a sustained controversy between the *Sentinel* and the *Pennsylvania Inquirer* in which Barker was given an embarrassing amount of publicity.

On the 8th of January, 1832, the usual Jackson dinner was given with the special feature, which Barker had aided in getting up, of presenting to President Jackson " a beautiful set of astral lamps, the chief material of which was the anthracite coal of Pennsylvania." [31] Barker's name appears prominently in the accounts of Jackson Day Festivities for 1833, 1834 and 1835. He delivered an oration at the 1835 dinner " in an eloquent and impressive manner—worthy both of the occasion and the reputation of the orator," [32] and was instrumental in sending to the General a memento of the affair in the form of a sword on which were engraved detailed pictures of the Battle of New Orleans.

The furor over Jackson's veto of the bank bill, in July, 1832, caused the President's Philadelphia sympathizers to hold a demonstration meeting in approval that was engineered by Barker and several of his friends.[33] When feeling again ran high over another crusade against the Bank, more gatherings were brought about by the same men, and a Committee of Correspondence was formed that addressed a series of four letters to the Democratic citizens of Pennsylvania through the columns of the *Daily Pennsylvanian*.[34] Barker, as a member of the Committee of Correspondence, appears to have been the author of all four letters together with a fifth one " vetoed as too strong " that was never printed. The manuscript of the fifth letter [35] is labeled " 5 letters to the People of Pennsylvania by J. N. B." in his own handwriting. The series is written in a

30 May 30, 1831.
31 *American Sentinel,* January 13, 1832.
32 *Daily Pennsylvanian,* January 9.
33 *Ibid.,* July 20.
34 March 22, April 5, 12, May 3, 1834.
35 Keys Collection.

facile, if somewhat elaborate style, easily to be identified as Barker's official manner. It is a partisan, well ordered, skillfully substantiated defense of Jackson and a savage, though none the less well informed, attack upon the United States Bank. The final letter appeals to the people to avoid entailing the freedom of their descendants to the spirit of aristocracy as represented in the bank and the party standing behind it. It is a cutting, swinging arraignment of Jackson's opponents, lauds him as the great friend of the people, goes back through history citing contests and events in the crises of the country to illustrate the selfish, despicable principles that threatened her independence and that in 1834 were once again by artfulness, fraud and the bank attempting to enslave her. It is, truly, an unrestrained challenge which if the committee had made it public, would have stung more of the opposition into action than it would have enlisted Democrats.

Barker's personal popularity, official position, inheritance and long association with Philadelphia community life identified him, during the decade in the Custom House, with other things than revenue collecting, political functions, and party advancement. Community welfare and charitable interests were not neglected. The first of February, 1830,[36] he had journeyed to Harrisburg with ten other citizens as a committee to petition the legislature to have the Pennsylvania Railroad place its terminus on the city side of the Schuylkill River "to avoid depriving the city of the accustomed trade," and was, for the second time, behind a movement to make Philadelphia the state capital "by the adoption of such measures as may justify the legislature in the choice of Philadelphia as the future seat of government." [37] The veterans of the Revolution deserved, he was convinced, the lasting gratitude of every citizen, and he himself aided any of them whenever opportunity offered. He secured a position at Fort Mifflin for

[36] *Philadelphia Gazette,* February 2.

[37] *Daily Pennsylvanian,* February 7, 1835.

Moses Smith by an appeal in his behalf to President Jackson,[38] and offered to write a biography of the Revolutionary hero, Andrew Wallace, to be accompanied by a portrait that the artist John Neagle agreed to paint, the proceeds of the joint work to be turned over to the veteran.[39] He helped in placing "contribution boxes in all steamboats in the Delaware and neighboring waters for the benefit of Robert Fulton's heirs." [40] Barker had heard Fulton explain his famous torpedoes in Washington years before, had sketched his life for Delaplaine, and honored him as a great genius of America. When the destruction of New York City was seriously threatened by a huge fire in December of 1835,[41] Barker came forward to serve in gathering funds that were dispatched to the sufferers of that tragedy. He was justly many times toasted as a philanthropist.

His connections with the drama and the theatre, while limited, were not wholly severed by public affairs in this period. December 20, 1829, he became one of the trustees of a "Theatrical Fund for Decayed Actors," as Durang puts it.[42] Rules and regulations for the government of the association were drawn up by a committee of five representing the Chestnut Street, Arch Street, and Walnut Street theatres. W. B. Wood was one of those who served but shortly withdrew "since the idea didn't suit his old fashioned propriety." [43] A performance of *Macbeth* was given for the fund at the Arch Street Theatre, March 26, 1830, by the corps of the three play houses "with the gratuitous services of Mr. Forrest" [44] who was also one of the trustees. The fund "failed here although something succeeded in New York."

38 Ms letter, March 11, 1830, Historical Society of Pennsylvania.

39 Ms letter of John Neagle, March 9, 1831, Historical Society of Pennsylvania.

40 *Hazard's Pennsylvania Register,* Vol. VI, September 4, 1830.

41 *Daily Pennsylvanian,* December 19.

42 Durang, *op. cit.,* Chap. 49.

43 *Ibid.*

44 *Philadelphia Gazette,* March 25.

Barker not only kept in touch with the drama in Philadelphia but corresponded with some of the New York group of playwrights as would seem to be evidenced in a letter of James Lawson enclosing, for Barker's perusal, a copy of his *Giordano*, which was about to appear at the Arch Street Theatre.[45] He was evidently regarded as one of the influential forces of Philadelphia's theatrical life. At the beginning of 1834 he appeared again in the theatrical notices as a dramatist with the revival of *Marmion* at the Arch Street Theatre with J. R. Scott in the title role.[46] Then, later that year, he joined the other Philadelphia playwrights, David Paul Brown, Robert Montgomery Bird, James McHenry and Richard Penn Smith, in giving a public dinner in honor of the English actor and dramatist, J. Sheridan Knowles. It was held in Masonic Hall on Chestnut Street and largely attended. Songs composed for the event by McHenry were sung and speeches were delivered by each of the dramatists, with the exception of Barker, and by several theatrical men and city officials.[47] Barker and these same "patrons of the Drama," as they were called, were the vital members of a committee to give the veteran actor and manager, W. B. Wood, a complimentary benefit performance. It took place January 11, 1836,[48] at the Chestnut Street Theatre with a success that practically turned it into a municipal testimony. Wood wrote[49] of the benefit that it "proved one of the most gratifying events of my life," and added a few lines later, "I was honored by the presence of one of the most brilliant audiences ever assembled. On this occasion the pit was furnished appropriately, and devoted wholly to the ladies, presenting a sight as novel as it was beautiful. None but an actor can appreciate a scene like this was, which in a moment throws into oblivion all recollections of anxieties, toils,

45 Ms letter, April 20, 1832, Historical Society of Pennsylvania.

46 *Daily Pennsylvanian,* January 4.

47 *Ibid.,* November 27, 1834.

48 *Ibid.,* January 13.

49 W. B. Wood, *Personal Recollections of the Stage,* pp. 400–401.

and modifications inseparable from a profession like ours. The following entertainment was offered:—' Three and a Deuce,' two acts of ' Venice Preserved,' ' John of Paris,' ' Antony's Oration,' a new song, and ' How to die for Love.' I was favored in these pieces with the valuable aid of Mr. Balls, Mr. J. Wallack, Mr. Abbot, Mrs. and Miss Watson, Mr. Wemyss, and Mr. Burton." It must have been a spectacular night.

It was not long after this, March 26, 1836, that Barker's earlier play, *How to Try a Lover,* written and published in 1817, but never before performed, was given three times with enthusiastic applause at the Arch Street Theatre under the new title *A Court of Love.*[50] Another revival of *Marmion* occurred March 29 of the following year, which was the last staging of one of his plays that Barker experienced while in Philadelphia.

In spite of other time-consuming affairs occasional poetry was on several instances produced by Barker during this era. The old theme of his Jacksonian admiration called forth a poem for the 8th of January celebration in 1829. This was a song, sung at the meeting in Masonic Hall, captioned " The Battle of New Orleans " and adapted to the revolutionary air " O Ye Nations." The descriptions of battle scenes are animated with echoes of the author's own experiences.[51] After a number of stanzas devoted to such scenes, the whole poem is swung into an application to the glory of Jackson, who, finally, is

> Like Washington, throned in the hearts of the nation
> The same in his virtue, the same in his station.

which song, sung in the enthusiasm of the anniversary by many war veterans and Democrats, must have had its effect.

An ode " To an Old Hickory—the Council Tree of the Tribe " was written for the 1830 meeting of the " Society for the Commemoration of the Landing of William Penn " in Washington Hall, October 25, at which " Upwards of 100 gentlemen were

50 See pp. 69–72.

51 *American Sentinel,* January 14.

present,"[52] Senators, the Postmaster General, Justices of the Supreme Court, the Mayor of New York and the American Minister to Madrid. Barker prefaced his ode with a brief exposition that is here reproduced, together with the poem, as exemplifying something as to his methods and procedure. The poem itself is pliant verse, calmly dignified in mood and quietly successful. Its application to " Old Hickory " Andrew Jackson is obvious.

" Having been honored by a request of the Society, through its committee, to furnish a poetical contribution to this celebration I could do no other than endeavour to comply with its wishes. The subjects immediately connected with the occasion being, however, limited, and somewhat trite from frequent use, I felt at a loss what theme to adopt; until happening to open Hazard's Register of Saturday, I observed a paragraph which appeared to offer all I could wish. We have often sung the glories of the *Elm.* I now purpose, in my humble way, to do homage to the *Hickory.* I allude, sir, to no *ordinary* Hickory, for in that case, although the hickory is deservedly ranked among the best productions of our soil—being not only in its noble aspect, highly ornamental, but, according to approved authors (Michaux, and others) of signal and extensive benefit both to the civilized and the savage, the white and the red man,—yet, it might not present itself on this *peculiar* occasion with any *special* pretensions. But this, sir, I repeat it, is no everyday production of nature, and will, I am confident, be found worthy to command our veneration. It is, moreover, strictly appropriate, being intimately associated with the very causes of our present festival, as the Society will acknowledge when I shall have read the following extract:

" ' Where Lancaster is now built, was once an Indian town, a hickory tree stood in its centre, not far from a spring under this tree the Council met, and it was from one of these councils that a deputation was sent to confer with William Penn at Shackamaxon.

[52] *Hazard's Pennsylvania Register,* VI, 330. The poem is here printed with the notice of the meeting.

The Indian nation was called Hickory, and the town was called Hickory, before Lancaster was laid out.—From *Hazard's Pennsylvania Register,* October 23, 1830.'

" I, of course, sir, take the truth of the tradition for granted, as poets, in like cases, are in duty bound to do; and use the agreeable license also, to address the subject of the ode, as still in existence; having no reason, indeed, to fear it is otherwise, and hoping, as I fervently do, that it is, and long may continue flourishing in full health and vigor." Then the ode:

Green in immortal verse, the sacred Elm
Yet blooms, unwithered o'er its hallowed site:—
And shall the flood of time thy memory whelm;
Its forest-brother! thou, whom, in thy might,
The storm breaks not, as, in thy towering height,
Thou bendest but erect again to be;
Looking with scorn upon the puny fight
Of adverse elements—not shaking thee,
In thy deep, steadfast root, majestic Hickory!

No; though alas not mine the gifted hand
To wake the living strain, the time is near
Thy worth shall swell the theme, while all the land
Shall to the plaudit turn the willing ear;
The red man in the shelter of thy arms,
Lessons of love and peace inclined to hear,
Pointing him to the path where war's alarms
Come not,—thought it was deck'd with all his wild-wood charms.

Then Fame shall mark, where thou its guardian stood,
A gallant nation met in council sage,
Securing present—seeking future good:
Prepared, if foes assailed, the war to wage
Preferring peace,—on the historic page
Stamped with thy character:—by nature strong,
Yet pliant to all good:—in youth and age,
Towering amid the clouds that darkly throng,
Proud—fearless to the last; of all the storm of wrong.

The centennial of Washington's birth was observed with a patriotic procession in 1832. And at the request of the city printers, with whom Barker was connected through his nephew, W. L. Barker, who had been a member of that profession,[53] he composed an ode for the "Printer's Society" and gave it the title "Birth Day of Washington." This, as at the time of the Lafayette reception in 1824, was distributed to the crowds from a wagon press as were several thousand copies of Washington's farewell address.[54] The day "when angels waved their golden wings, and Washington was born" was first depicted, then the permanency of the brilliance of Washington's name, the homage of grateful millions, and as a culmination the blessings of the people "on their patriot sage, their hero, father, friend!"

At that time there existed a long established club of Philadelphia gentlemen known as "The Fishing Company of the State in Schuylkill" devoted to social amenities as well as to fishing. Their rustic club house was referred to as "The Castle" and was located on the Schuylkill river not far from the city limits. The centennial of "The Fishing Company" fell on May 1, 1832, when numerous guests, Barker and his fellow dramatist R. P. Smith among them, were entertained at a banquet "in the hall of the Castle decorated with bowers, trophies, and evergreens." Here Barker "recited" a poem prepared for the occasion headed "Ode—For the Centennial Celebration of the Foundation of the State in Schuylkill, May 1st, 1832," afterwards printed in *Poulson's Advertiser*[55] and in a history of the club.[56] The ode is a neat abridgment of the past of the Fishing Company and the noted characters and events associated with it. It is elaborately buttressed by full footnotes to the historical

53 *Democratic Press,* October 2, 1824.

54 *American Sentinel,* February 24.

55 May 5, 1832.

56 *A History of the Schuylkill Fishing Company of the State in Schuylkill,* Philadelphia, 1889. Pp. 121–136 contain the ode and a detailed picture of the banquet similar to the account in *Poulson's.*

references that, if contributing little to the poetry as such, reveal Barker's thorough knowledge of American history and traditions. His genuine love for the past gave him a deep concern for truthful accuracy in its exploitation.

It was a long-standing local habit, in those days, for the carriers of the newspapers of Philadelphia to address the subscribers on the first of each year through the verse of one or another of the literati of the city. This was usually distributed as a broadside and afterwards reprinted in the paper. It was in keeping with this tradition that Barker was the author of the "Address of the Carriers of the Pennsylvanian"[57] for 1836. This gayly satirizes the political figures and trends of the year in harmony with the Democratic politics of both the paper and the writer. It is good political verse the tone of which is sufficiently established in this opening portion—

Usher'd in by old custom, the Carrier attends,
On this holiday morning on patrons and friends,
With a wish from his heart, of a happy New Year,
And a lay from his muse, which she begs you to hear:
But if rather sententious or flippant she grows,
On your candor her cause and her carrier she throws,
With the hope that at New Year, 'tis not out of season
To mingle a mince-meat of pied rhyme and reason—
A kind of an olla podrida of rhymes—
For what but a medley can figure *the times!*

Verse for the annuals of the day was first written by Barker in 1825 with the beginning of the publication of *The Atlantic Souvenir, a Christmas and New Year's Offering* by Carey and Lea of Philadelphia. "It is stated in the neat preface," so a notice of it ran,[58] "to the Atlantic Souvenir that every article in the volume is from the pen of some one of several Americans who

[57] *Daily Pennsylvanian,* January 2, 1836. Literary Pamphlets, Ridgway Library Collection.

[58] *Democratic Press,* November 25, 1825.

have acquired celebrity as writers both at home and abroad. The names of Paulding, Bryant, Sedgwick, Barker and Waln, are mentioned." As, however, nearly all of the selections are anonymous for this number, which is the volume dated for 1826, it has not been possible accurately to identify Barker's specific contribution. From the nature of their subject matter "A Legend of the Forest,"[59] a narrative poem on an Indian myth, and "Freedom," concerning Greece and her independence, seem the most likely to be his. In the later volumes, although some of those for subsequent years are missing, the authors are indicated —"Little Red Riding Hood" by Barker in the 1828 number of *The Souvenir*, was based on an engraving from Sir T. Laurence's painting on the subject. Many of the poems in the annuals were built around engravings the editors wished to use as illustrations. These books were souvenirs of art as well as of letters. Barker himself was exceedingly fond of engravings and had an extensive collection, a few of which are still in the possession of his granddaughter, Miss Josephine Keys. This particular poem is in the guise of a dialogue between a mother and a small daughter over the hidden, true moral of the Riding Hood story. Love is the wolf, it develops, which thought leads into crisp social satire and some effective descriptive poetry of nature.[60] This latter is rich in detail bringing to mind another poetical work of Barker's about which no more is known than "Being botanically inclined, and fond of rural description, I had the material prepared for a book of poetico-prose botany, to be beautifully christened the *Circle of the Seasons*—when, by heavens, there is published in England not only a *Book of the Seasons*, but an identical *Circle of the Seasons!*"[61]

The 1829 *The Atlantic Souvenir* contained three Barker poems, each taking its origin in an engraving. "Love

59 P. 104.
60 Pp. 97–101.
61 Dunlap, *op. cit.*, p. 377.

Asleep "[62] is in the same vein as the social comedy in *Tears and Smiles.* It is woven about an Italian tale, suitable to the engraved illustration, of a man hating above all things to see a woman sleep who, coming upon his love in that condition, promptly deserts her while she dreams—when

> 'Tis not thought
> Angelica went mad—of all God's creatures,
> A coxcomb is the thing soonest forgotten.

It has "a sprinking of fun over it" that glints most entertainingly. "The Power of Love," the second of the three, was reprinted in *Specimens of Metropolitan Literature,*[63] and, in part, in the *Lady's Amaranth,*[64] and is well typified in the quatrain—

> Beware then, lady, no one knows
> What courser Love may choose to try,
> The storm—the odour of the rose,
> The dragon—or the dragon fly.[65]

The third poem, "Hesitation,"[66] is a charming love song on the revealing quality of modest fears and doubtful hesitation in love.

"The Three Sisters"[67] and "The Gipseying Party,"[68] both again for engraved illustrations, are in *The Souvenir* for 1830. The former of these is a light, airy song offering a parallel between three girls and three roses, touches the ephemeral quality of both and draws a lesson for the sisters from the flowers. It was reproduced in the *American Sentinel.*[69] "The Gipseying Party" lauds the pleasures of simple nature, narrates a rural stroll, describes the plain strength and beauty of homespun char-

62 Pp. 16–22.

63 Sometimes entitled *The Philadelphia Book,* Philadelphia, 1836.

64 Philadelphia, Vol. II, January 19, 1839.

65 P. 119.

66 P. 207.

67 P. 130.

68 P. 87.

69 September 23, 1829.

acters and regrets the artificialities and stuffy stirring of the city. It is a sincere appreciation of the out-of-doors. It again appeared afterwards in *Godey's Lady's Book* [70] and the *American Sentinel* [71] in 1832. Music, love and poetry are the three outstanding themes, singly and in combination, of four other poems for the 1831 and 1832 editions of *The Souvenir*. "The Minstrel" [72] has a light ironic touch in its address to a girl musician that by contrast heightens the fascination and charm of music for Barker that permeate the whole. The "spirit of blest poesy" is invoked in "Arcadia," in the same volume,[73] to carry the poet—

> Back, from this artificial age,
> Hence, from this cold and sordid clime,
> Where mortals scorn the poet's rage,
> And honest poverty is crime,
> Speed, to where nature wanders blithe and free,
> To Arcady, to Arcady.

His wish is granted—

> 'Tis won, the golden land is won,
> In golden numbers sung.

He then wanders among the storied places and people of Greek mythology until—

> Spirit, I must back again
> To the haunts of worldly men
> Wonder not this lovely sight,
> To my cot should speed my flight.
> It may have a homelier dress,
> But it holds my shepherdess;
> And with love to aid and you,

70 February 1, 1832.
71 February 29.
72 Pp. 194–196, 1831.
73 Pp. 210–216.

Bland magicians, it may do:
With love and you, the wilderness may be
An Arcady, a golden Arcady.

The change in mood from one of wearied depression to a less fretted, happier one, brought by the consolation of poetry, is admirably developed. Also in *The Souvenir* for 1831 is the short poem " Los Musicas "[74] in the verses of which " harmony, friendship, and love " are found infinitely preferable to gold, glory or " the vapour of fame." There is, then, the one poem, " Lord Byron in Early Youth,"[75] that represents Barker in the same annual in 1832. This extenuates the blighted youth and beauty of Byron, is filled with sympathy for his misery and admiration for his genius; and, in view of the Byronic influence upon verses such as " Love Asleep," is interesting and enlightening. This one stanza, however, elucidates the essential reason for the admiration and the complete consistency of Barker's beliefs:

But lo, the earthquake of the soul had pass'd,
And thy freed spirit look'd on brighter skies;
The wail of suffering Greece came on the blast,
And glory offered thee her brightest prize.
Byron, 'tis thine! amidst a nation's cries,
Thou sank'st immortal on thy field of fame
Champion of freedom—thy pure name defies
The touch of time: death sanctifies the claim,
And join'd to thy own Greece, will flourish Byron's name.

The canons of freedom and democracy, the beauties of nature and poetry, and the spirit of love, music and friendship are the guiding principles weaving through this verse for the annuals that link it with the drama, prose and personality of Barker. He is nothing, if not consistent to his belief in his ideals.

74 P. 324.
75 P. 140.

VIII.

WASHINGTON THROUGH THE CHANGING ADMINISTRATIONS

THE appointment of Barker to be First Comptroller of the Treasury was made partly for political reasons, but partly, also, in recognition of his real ability. The " Theory of Rotation in Office " frantically advocated by the Philadelphia office seekers, the necessity of taking care of former Governor Wolf of Pennsylvania, who was dissatisfied in the treasury, were factors. Barker had been thorough and effective in the Philadelphia Custom House and had shown his skill in handling all sorts of political situations. Then, too, he was a firm friend of James Buchanan's and still a real power in the Democratic party in Pennsylvania. In dignity, executive scope and ranking the transfer to Washington was a promotion—in salary a setback. It must have been with somewhat conflicting motives that Van Buren had acted.

After Barker's removal to Washington his name yet remained an influence in Philadelphia. At the usual Democratic festivities of the 4th of July, he was invited to participate in the celebration as one of the party leaders. Unable to get away from the Treasury, he forwarded a toast that was to " The People: They are a majority everywhere, and of right should everywhere govern. When the *few* bear sway, it is a proof of the baseness of the *many*."[1] To which the company through the committee in charge, replied with the sentiment, " James N. Barker, Esq., our friend and fellow citizen—a talented and faithful scion from a genuine Democratic stock; like his ancestor he prefers *principles* to *interest*. In him confidence cannot be misplaced."[2] The " principles " and " interest " refer apparently to the " Ro-

1 *Daily Pennsylvanian,* July 9, 1838.

2 *Ibid.*

tation in Office" and the transfer to Washington. Jackson's Day, also, was customarily a time of party caucus in Philadelphia, as well as an anniversary of the Battle of New Orleans. Again the leading Democrats of the state foregathered and Barker, in 1839, was asked to attend. The following exchange of opinion took place as a consequence of Barker's detainment in the capital. "Old Pennsylvania," Barker wrote, "She can always give her enemies an Orleans defeat; surprise and check them in December, to amaze and disperse them in January,"[3] while the meeting answered, "James N. Barker who neither in politics nor war ever feared an enemy or betrayed a friend."[4] Although these are more or less polite amenities, they generally occurred only in cases where the men concerned were felt to be high in the councils of the party.

The duties of Barker's new position were intricate, and while he was already familiar with the general revenue system through his Philadelphia experiences as collector, it required much energy and time to adjust himself and become familiar with the business of the comptroller's office. There were many decisions to be made regarding the classification of imports, the exact application of the tariff laws, law suits and seizures of goods.[5] A general policy had to be developed and set by the new Comptroller to guide him in his relationship with the numerous collectors, all of whom, at that time, were directly under the detailed supervision of his office. Barker, with his habitual thoroughness, was desirous of a more unified and efficient system. He wrote to the assistant collector in Philadelphia, who had served under him, with the hope "that our united labors may be of some use in providing a proper and uniform practice."[6] There was, further, some difficulty in untangling the accounts of the Philadelphia

[3] *Ibid.*, January 14.

[4] *Daily Pennsylvanian*, January 14.

[5] See *Letter Book, Correspondence with the Departments*, for 1838, 1839, and 1840, Philadelphia Custom House.

[6] *Letter Book, Correspondence with the Departments*, August 22, 1838.

Custom House. The reports of the new collector, Governor Wolf, who had exchanged offices with Barker, seemed "to need explanation" of "discrepancies."[7] A question as to the proper transfer of funds and treasury notes to the credit of Barker as Philadelphia collector arose in an effort to close the affairs of his regime in that position. The Treasurer of the United States was brought into the discussion,[8] and after a good deal of irritation and correspondence the matter was ultimately adjusted. The welfare of the clerks who had so long served under him in the Custom House at Philadelphia was likewise still of concern to him. "The interest," so he wrote to Collector Wolf, "I very naturally feel for the Custom House at Philadelphia, will I hope justify me in an expression of my opinion in regard to the provision inserted in the relief section [of a recent law governing revenue service] for the benefit of the clerks in the office of the collector."[9] This opinion was in favor of an increase in salary and he had gone beyond the requisites of his official duties in presenting it.

Personal inclination and family loyalty had caused Barker to bring with him to Washington the two relatives who had been appointed by him to positions in the Philadelphia Custom House. These two gentlemen, B. F. Rogers and J. B. North, were his brothers-in-law, and were both given clerkships in the comptroller's office[10] and remained in government employ at least until 1859. This shift, moreover, helped Barker to a partial settlement of his domestic problem, especially as it had to do with his small daughter. He and his children made their home with the North family on the east side of New Jersey Avenue between A. and B. Streets[11] where Rachel Jackson, usually called Mary Barker, was under the care and direction of her

[7] *Ibid.*, September 29, and December 11.

[8] *Ibid.*,

[9] *Ibid.*, January 14, 1839.

[10] *Register of the United States Government,* 1841, p. 15.

[11] A. Reitzel, *Washington Directory,* 1843, p. 178.

aunt. The deep affection and companionship between Barker and his children show a facet of his personality that adds further to its appeal. The charm and revealing nature of the following letter to his small daughter, illustrates the situation, and exemplifies something, also, as to the adaptability of his prose style. The note was addressed " Miss R. J. M. Barker, Care of Aunty " and written with printed letters so as to be very legible.[12]

WASHINGTON, August 10, 1839.

My dear daughter,

I hear with more and more pleasure of your improvement in health. I shall expect to see you actually fat and rosy. And then how you must run about to wear out so many shoes!

I received your present from the Lily pond—and thank you very heartily for thinking of me and sending me such sweet and beautiful flowers: I only wish I had been with you to pull them.

Do you still continue to take the surf so boldly? I should like to see you of all things.

Your brothers are all well—only poor Jimmy has the tooth ache sometimes in the night, and then he kicks worse than ever. They all send pockets full of kisses.

Take great care of yourself, whether in bathing, riding, running, skipping, jumping, sitting, standing, sleeping or walking.

Be still a good girl, and God bless you.

Your affectionate father

J. N. BARKER

Your friends all send love. Caroline Towson, and Louisa desire particularly to be kindly remembered.

I send you, as remembrances, two flowers from your own little garden—a *pensée* is one that means thoughts—the other is from your virgin bower.

Again, bless you, my dear Rachel. J. N. B.

Miss Rachel J. M. Barker.

Barker's position as second ranking executive in the Treasury [13] was recognized as of both political and social importance,

12 Ms letter, Keys Collection.

13 *Register of the United States Government,* 1841.

at least as indicated by the use of his name in school, social, and business notices and advertisements in the Washington papers. From these it would seem his daughter was soon sent to a Miss Breschard's "Boarding and Day School for Young Ladies," [14] and his sons enrolled in the "Washington Academy for Young Gentlemen" [15] and later sent to the "Select, Classical and English Academy" in 1846.[16]

With the election of Harrison and Tyler in 1840, Barker's political future looked dark. A horde of eager office-seekers flooded the capital in 1841 clamoring for the official scalps of all good Democrats.[17] Notwithstanding President Harrison's reiterated declarations of retaining all efficient office holders, geat numbers were dismissed, and Barker was removed as Comptroller April 19, 1841,[18] or thereabouts. A five months interim followed in which, evidently, Barker for the first time since 1817 was without official position of any sort. Vice-President Tyler upon ascension to the Presidency, however, turned Democrat and appointed Barker, who was not only a Democrat but a personal acquaintance through the President's brother, William Tyler, as Acting Comptroller of the Treasury September 14, 1841.[19] The selection was widely noticed as showing the Presidential drift, and the *Daily Globe* contained an article to the effect that

"It is with much pleasure we see the restoration of that faithful and able officer to the post of First Comptroller of the Treasury, the

14 *Daily Globe,* Washington, July 30, 1842.

15 *Daily Globe,* February 6, 1843.

16 Washington, *Daily Union,* January 12.

17 See files of the *Daily Globe* for March and April, 1841.

18 Files of the Division of Appointments, Treasury Department, give this date, but the Washington *National Intelligencer* announced his successor's appointment April 16, 1841; while the *Daily Union* in referring back to the event on June 14, 1845 states that "On the 6th day of April, while the deceased President was reposing in his coffin, James N. Barker was removed from the office of Comptroller of the Treasury."

19 Official commission, Keys Collection.

duties of which he has heretofore discharged with so much credit to himself and advantage to the country.

"Major Barker was one of the gallant defenders of his country during the last war, and no man of his grade won, at that day, a more enviable reputation. Since that time his firm, fearless, and honest conduct has gained him an unusual share of the regard of his friends and the respect of his opponents. Selected by the greedy office hunters who surrounded General Harrison, and who controlled his better impulses, as a sacrifice to the Moloch of party, he is now fitly and properly restored under the juster auspices of President Tyler." [20]

In the meantime Henry Clay and the Whigs had declared war on Tyler for his desertion to the Democrats; so when the President sent Barker's nomination as regular First Comptroller of the Treasury to the Senate on December 30, 1841,[21] they seized the opportunity to annoy him. The nomination was referred to the Committee on Finance the same day,[22] and was reported from the committee February 10, 1842, when Senator Buchanan,[23] who was steering the matter for Barker, had the consideration of the question postponed until the next day. A debate ensued, when again Buchanan, evidently foreseeing defeat and maneuvering for time, tried for another postponement of a week. He was defeated in this, and the nomination was rejected [24] on a strictly party alignment 17 to 23.[24] Buchanan then, in an effort to save Barker as much as possible, was successful in having the following motion approved. "Resolved, That the nomination of James N. Barker as Comptroller of the Treasury has not been rejected by the Senate on account of any belief that his official conduct in the case of the Swartwout defalcation [25] was negli-

20 September 25, 1841.

21 *Journal of the Executive Proceedings of the Senate,* VI, 3.

22 *Ibid.,* p. 8.

23 *Journal of the Executive Proceedings of the Senate,* VI, 25.

24 *Ibid.,* pp. 26–27.

25 Samuel Swartwout was Collector of Customs at New York, who during the years 1830–1838 stole about $1,225,000 of the revenue and absconded

gent or improper." Senator Franklin Pierce then took a hand in Barker's behalf in having the injunction of secrecy removed from the vote. Both Democratic and Whig press vented their feelings with enthusiasm. The *Daily Globe*, the dominant Democratic sheet of Washington, under the heading "Rejection of James N. Barker"[26] had this, and a great deal more to say:

"The Whig party in the Senate signalized on Friday last, their consistent adherence to the doctrine of the Roman Consul, by acting when in power in a manner directly at variance with their professions before attaining it. This excellent officer and worthy man was expelled from a place of which he discharged the duties with exemplary fidelity, because he was a Democrat. A brave soldier in the last war, to whose merits the amplest testimony has been given by every officer with whom he served; a patriot in every sense of the word; a public servant whose integrity in the most responsible offices of trust has never been impeached; himself mild, forbearing and considerate in the warmest periods of political contest—it might have been supposed that the vengeance of Federalism would have been satiated with its numerous victims without sacrificing him upon its unholy altar. But Mr. Barker had not swerved from the fearless avowal of his political opinions; he is a Democrat of the old fashioned school; he is cherished by the Democracy of Pennsylvania, who have honored him more than once with their confidence; this was ground broad enough for the whole party to unite upon, and accordingly he was sacrificed to the spirit of party.

"We must, however, admit our conviction, that there was something more meant in this proscription than a demonstration of fixed hostility to the Democracy. Mr. Barker's was an appointment made by President Tyler. He was strongly recommended by Mr. Forward, who had while Comptroller, availed himself of Mr. Barker's experience in that office, and knew his qualifications for the trust.

just after Barker was made Comptroller. Barker was unfairly accused by the opposition of laxity in checking the New York accounts when as a matter of fact all the irregularities had occurred while he was still in Philadelphia. *Daily Globe,* February 24, 1842.

[26] February 14, 1842.

We have heard, moreover, that Mr. Barker had, during the war, placed a brother of Mr. Tyler under obligations, by preserving his life; and the nomination was, therefore, one of grateful personal acknowledgment, at the same time that it was an acknowledgment of the well tried official capacity and worth of the individual presented. It was, no doubt, intended also as a manifestation on the part of the President, of his purpose to tolerate at least some of the Democrats, and in a slight degree countenance the declaration of his Inaugural Address."

Barker's old friend, the *Daily Pennsylvanian* of Philadelphia, also came to his defense, the same day,[27] with like statements, and was irritated into a final utterance on the case when the "*Independent*," "a Clay organ, issued at Washington," launched "a furious attack upon Major Barker, which, from the gross misrepresentation thrown out to palliate the conduct of the Senate, demanded a reply." [28] From this reply, it appears that the *Independent* accused Barker of "gross neglect" of duty and general roguery, which the *Pennsylvanian* found easy to refute and to turn back upon the Whigs. The *Daily Globe* gleefully reprinted the reply,[29] and the dispute, after a few more brief references, gave way to other contention.

After continuing as Acting Comptroller until at least March 12, 1842,[30] Barker was out of the Treasury Department for the second time, and unconnected with government service. This retirement lasted just short of six months, until in September 2, 1842, he was appointed clerk in the office of the Secretary of the Treasury, a position open to direct appointment by the Secretary.[31] This was the best post in the Treasury not under Senate approval, and more lucrative than any in the Comptroller's office,

27 February 14, 1842.

28 February 23, 1842.

29 February 24, 1842.

30 *Letter Book, Correspondence and Circulars,* 1842–1843, March 12, 1842.

31 *Executive Documents, 27th Congress, 3d Session,* V, 2, document no. 160.

which latter fact may account for the transfer from that division of the department. Here in the Secretary's office, at all events, he placed his valuable experience at the service of the department and was assistant to the Secretary of the Treasury until at least 1846.[32]. The official position of Assistant Secretary of the Treasury was a different office not established until March 3, 1849.[33] Barker remained in the Treasury Department until 1858, the year of his death.

He took part in many of the official ceremonies including those of inducting the Polk administration in 1845. As a member of the Capitol Hill Democratic Association he was one of a group to welcome the President and Vice-President elect upon their arrival at the capital, February 15,[34] and served, along with his brother-in-law, B. F. Rogers, as one of the managers of the "Democratic Inaugural Ball," at which function he also acted as one of the reception committee.[35] He was chosen one of the peace makers in an attempt to adjust the ill feeling that arose over a hot dispute between the supporters of the "Democratic Inaugural Ball" and one called the "National Inaugural Ball,"[36] both of which were held. For the occasion of the inaugural parade and ceremonies he was created Deputy Marshal of the District of Columbia, March 3d,[37] and was designated as one of six Democrats "to attend ex-President Tyler, Mrs. Tyler and Acting ex-Vice-President Maugrum from Carusis' to the Democratic Inauguration Ball at 11 o'clock on the 4th of March."[38]

His presence, as one of the committee of arrangements, at a

32 J. T. Towers, *Washington City Directory,* 1846, p. 90; R. Mayo, *United States Fiscal Department,* 1847, recommendations printed at the end of Vol. II.

33 Bulletin, Form 70073, issued by the Treasury Department, 1921.

34 *Daily Globe,* February 15.

35 *Ibid.,* March 3, 1845.

36 *Ibid.,* January 28.

37 *Daily Globe,* of that date.

38 *Ibid.,* March 3, 1845.

public dinner given by the citizens of Washington to Lieut. Col. May, July 12, 1847,[39] must have carried him back to numerous others so frequent in his days in Philadelphia when as official, orator, or poet he had done his share in the successful expression of the community or national feelings of the people.

The news of the success of the French Revolution of 1848 was enthusiastically received in the United States, consequent upon which many public demonstrations of approval occurred. In Washington feeling was keen, and on April 10, 1848, at a town meeting the preliminaries for a huge demonstration were undertaken.[40] Barker was placed on the general committee, and his son, William, was one of the assistant marshals of the extensive parade that, with " speeches at the east portico of the capitol,"[41] featured the celebration on April 24th. The government offices were closed, the House and Senate adjourned and all official Washington including the Vice-President and cabinet members, participated—

" The procession," to quote the *Daily Union*,[42] " was graced by a corps of printers, who carried with them, upon a large car drawn by four horses, a printing press, which threw off copies of the following beautiful verses, composed by Major Barker of the Treasury Department.

ODE TO FRANCE

Air—the Marseillaise

Again, O France, thy star of glory
Bursts on the world's enraptur'd sight;
Again illumes thy ancient story,
And marks thy onward path of light.
No adverse gleam again shall pale it;
No demons riding on the storm,

39 *Ibid.*, July 12.
40 *Daily Union,* April 13.
41 *Daily Union,* April 25.
42 *Ibid.*

Again shall its fair face deform,
Or in ensanguin'd clouds shall veil it.

Chorus Arm, arm, who dare be free—strike, strike for liberty
March on—march on, for Freedom's won by all who dare
be free.

O France, from thee enfranchis'd nations
Shall draw their new-born freedom's plan;
And learn from thee, whate'er their stations,
The *duties* with the *rights* of man.
Vengeance no more shall mercy smother—
The axe still following on the lance
But man shall learn from generous France
To spare his prostrate, vanquish'd brother.

Chorus Arm, arm, who dare be free, etc.

Already, lo! all Europe rising,
While Tyrants from their thrones are hurled—
O Liberty! thy blessings prizing,
At length thou'st welcomed by a world!
Man can no longer monsters cherish;
But, like the angry northern *Bear,*
They crouch within their savage lair,
Or on the hunter's javelin perish!

Chorus Arm, arm, who dare be free, etc.

This was read before the cabinet of President Polk and favorably noticed in the Philadelphia *Daily Pennsylvanian,*[43] and the *Baltimore Sun,*[44] the Washington correspondent of the former thinking that "The only thing really thrilling in the whole affair, was the poem of Major J. N. Barker. It is a beautiful thing. . . ." The idea of the wagon press was unquestionably Barker's suggestion drawn from the two previous instances in Philadelphia when odes of his were similarly distributed. His

43 April 28, 1848.
44 April 25, 1848.

verse, plainly, is once again good occasional poetry with most of the traits of his former work. The freely flowing, applicable style, the martial challenge on behalf of freedom, and the eulogistic treatment of liberty are unchanged. His poetical gifts had neither faded nor advanced.

The organization of the "Officers of the War of 1812" had to some degree been accomplished before 1849. In that year, however, a meeting was called February 28, "for the purpose of taking measures for testifying their respect for General Taylor, the President elect."[45] Barker, in keeping with his usual fate in such things, was placed on a committee of five to make suggestions and draw resolutions. The results, in the following form, were adopted:

"1. Resolved, That, hailing with thrilling interest the election of Zacharay Taylor, our associate in arms in the war of 1812, the third selection from our ranks, to a station without equal in the government of the world, we form an association to accompany him from the Capitol of the nation to the mansion of the Executive, on Monday, the 5th of March 1849.

"2. Resolved, That Colonel Todd, General Gratiat, Colonel Gardiner, Colonel Alston, Major Barker, and Major Camp be a committee to take suitable measures for ascertaining at what time the President elect, after he shall have been inducted into office, will receive the felicitations of the officers of the war of 1812.

"3. Resolved, That the officers of the navy and marine corps in the War of 1812 be invited to unite in the testimony of respect contemplated by the preceding resolutions."[46]

They were received by the President at 2 o'clock on the day of inauguration, March 5, when a complimentary address was delivered and answered, and "The President then mingled with great courtesy and cordiality among his ancient associates, and gratified them by some sportive remarks introduced with admir-

[45] *Daily Union,* March 4, 1849.

[46] *Ibid.,* March 4.

able taste." [47] Mrs. Madison was then visited, another address was made and acknowledged followed by disbandment. These veterans had come to Barker's assistance,[48] at the period of his difficulties in Tyler's time, and with their improved organization were, unquestionably, an influence in Barker's retention in office through another change in administration. Barker, on the other hand, had been associated in the Historical Society of Pennsylvania [49] with the new Secretary of the Treasury, W. M. Meredith, in earlier years, and may have been retained partly for that reason. The competition for office, anyhow, was severe, and in one case there were more than 100 applicants for a vacant $1100 clerkship in the Treasury.[50] Retention of office by him at this era practically meant permanent immunity for Barker.

The national gold fever growing out of the California discovery took the outlet in Washington, during 1849, of the "Washington City and California Mining Association." Two of Barker's sons, William and James, at once joined [51] and went West. They were in California in 1851,[52] remaining there until some time in 1853 when William was appointed clerk as from California, in the office of the Secretary of the Treasury,[53] likely securing that position through his father's influence.

On December 17, 1850, Barker's daughter, Mary, married Richard B. Keys of Baltimore [54] and went to live in that city where her husband was in business. Barker soon developed the habit of frequent visits to Baltimore.[55] With his daughter's de-

47 *Ibid.,* March 11.

48 Anonymous biographical sketch, n.d. (1858), Keys Collection.

49 *Charter and By-Laws of the Historical Society of Pennsylvania,* Philadelphia, 1880.

50 *Daily Union,* April 5, 1849.

51 *Ibid.,* March 31.

52 Ms letter, J. N. Barker to his daughter, January 9, 1851, Keys Collection.

53 *Register of the United States Government,* 1853.

54 *Daily Union,* December 20.

55 Ms letter of J. N. Barker to his daughter, January 9, 1851, Keys Collection.

parture he had left the North's home and lived at a boarding house on C. Street.[56] The letters of those days once more bring out the charming, domestic side of his personality. He was fascinated when a granddaughter, Aline, was born and delighted in his correspondence in referring to her. This extract is in the usual tone of his notes.

"My little journey was accomplished without accident. Seated in a snug corner of the car, I was transported in imagination, back to the quiet room in St. Charles Street. With the interesting scene before me, of the smiling mother and lovely daughter—and happy father—and tender grandma—and careful nurse, I arrived in C. Street in time to take my seat at the tea table, surrounded by the tittering girls and merry wives of our house, all congratulating me upon my being a grandfather! I fear I *must* get a white wig to be in true character, and frighten off the women." [57]

Verse making had not been entirely abandoned as in another, slightly earlier letter, October 31, 1851, he wrote "Pour la *cadeau*. I enclose herewith my humble offering in the shape of a couple of stanzas in the Byronian form—which I preferr'd as best adapted to the subject. When I assure you that it flowed fresh from my heart, I hope you will accept it with all its faults." [58] This has not survived but hints, at least, at a family interest in literature that is borne out by other suggestions and the family tradition as to Mrs. Keys's composition of short stories and the poetry of Wade Van Buren Barker, the youngest of the playwright's sons. His son John was a professional artist.

In connection with a Jackson Day dinner in Philadelphia in 1838, Barker had stated, in a letter to the committee, "I have never, that I can recollect, been absent from the festive board on its anniversary, nor can the day ever recur, while I have life, without awakening in my bosom emotions of just pride as an

56 Ms letter, December 16, n.d. (1851), Keys Collection.

57 *Ibid.*

58 Ms letter, Keys Collection.

American."[59] That almost life-long habit was still alive in 1854 when on January 8th he attended the annual Jacksonian banquet in Washington and gave the company the following toast so very indicative of his unchanging ideals—

> "As one of the great family of nations, the United States may never forget, in view of their foreign relations, that our warmest sympathies naturally belong to those who are gallantly contending for their independence and liberties."[60]

As a friend of James Buchanan's and the staunchest of Democrats as well, Barker had an active share in the inauguration of 1857. More than the customary stress was put upon the splendor of the entire ceremonies. A "Grand Inauguration Ball, for the Benefit of the Poor of Washington City" was held on March 3, Barker being one of the managers.[61] The President-elect was present and the affair was both fashionable and elaborate. Barker was, additionally, a marshal of the immense procession the next day—and a manager of what actually was a second inaugural ball, but the official one, designated as "The National Inauguration Ball." This in pomp and circumstance overshadowed all of the other festivities. Barker with that event ended his long career as an official of public functions.

During the closing years of his life, Barker boarded, as did his sons, at the corner of Pennsylvania Avenue and Sixth Street.[62] It was there that he was taken ill with pneumonia at the beginning of March, 1858, and died Tuesday the 9th of that same month. After funeral services in Washington, his body was brought to Philadelphia and buried in Laurel Hill Cemetery[63] at 11 o'clock on March 16.

The majority of the Philadelphia, Baltimore, and Washington

59 *Daily Pennsylvanian,* January 12.

60 *Daily Union,* January 13.

61 *Ibid.,* files for February and March contain the details.

62 *Boyd's Washington and Georgetown Directory,* 1858, pp. 27–28.

63 Records of the Laurel Hill Cemetery Company for lots 71 and 81.

newspapers contained comment upon Barker's death. Four Washington papers, in addition, carried this tribute:

TRIBUTE OF RESPECT

At a meeting of the clerks attached to the office of the Secretary of the Treasury convened March 10, 1858, the following resolutions were unanimously adopted.

Res. That we learned with the deepest sorrow of the decease of our associate and friend Maj. J. N. Barker which occurred at his residence in this city on Tuesday.

Res. That the amenity of manners, the social disposition, and kindness of heart, uniformly exhibited during his long service in the department, have created in our breasts the warmest feelings of attachment, while for his excellent and unblemished character through life we cherish the highest respect and veneration.

Res. That the many and important duties confided in him during his long and useful career have always been so efficiently and satisfactorily performed that we deplore the death as a public loss, while we mourn for the departure of a valued friend and companion.

Res. That we tender to his afflicted family our sincere sympathy for their bereavement, and participate in their sorrow at this loss, and that a copy of these resolutions be transmitted to them." [64]

[64] *Daily Union,* March 12, 1858.

IX

TEARS AND SMILES

IN an extended letter to William Dunlap, presented in full in the *History of the American Theatre*, Barker gives the following account of the origin and production of *Tears and Smiles:*

" *Tears and Smiles*, a comedy, in five acts, was written between the 1st of May and 12th of June, 1806. The idea of writing was suggested at a dinner of the fishing company, at their ancient castle on the Schuylkill, on which august occasion you yourself were a guest. The topic happened to be Breck's *Fox Chase*, which had been first acted on the preceding night. Manager Warren, who was present, asked me to enter the lists as a dramatist, and Jefferson put in for a Yankee character. By-the-way, such a Yankee as I drew! I wonder what Hackett would say to it. The truth is, I had never even seen a Yankee at the time. . . . *Tears and Smiles* was cast with the whole strength of the company: Warren, Wood, Cain, Jefferson, Blissett, Mills, McKenzie, Bray, and Mesdames Melmoth, Wood, Woodham, Francis, Jefferson. It was first acted March 4th, 1807, to a brilliant audience, and with complete success. Notwithstanding, I must confess that one of the deities of the gallery, where I had ensconced me, did fall fast asleep (O all ye gods!) in the second act. Nay, others appeared likely to follow his example, during the sentimental dialogue, and were perhaps only kept awake by the expectation of seeing 'that funny fellow, Jeff, again.' Never did I hail a 'funny fellow' with so much glee as on that eventful night. The prologue was kindly undertaken by Wood, who began in his most lofty manner,

With swelling port, imperious, and vain,

and there he stopped, at a dead fault. After in vain endeavouring to recall what was to follow, he addressed the audience:—

'Upon my soul, ladies and gentlemen, I am so unaccustomed to this kind of speaking, that I must beg,' &c., &c., in his peculiar, janty way, and with his usual happy effect. The piece was announced for repetition on the next night, the author was 'trotted out,' and ambled through the lobbies and boxes, and the booksellers made proposals—what a triumph for a tyro! . . . On the second night, being in the green-room, several of the ladies complained, on coming off, that they were put out in their parts by the loud and impertinent remarks from one of the stage boxes. My course was instantly adopted. I went around to the box, and calling out one of the gentlemen, made such an expostulation as had the desired effect. The conduct of those persons had been so flagrantly indecent as to draw upon them sounds of disapprobation from several parts of the house. They were certain witlings about town—Samuel Ewing, a lawyer, was one—who, induced by the reputation the piece had gained on the first night, to lay aside their habitual apathy towards American productions, were now aroused only to malignant feeling, as I was neither politically nor socially of their set."

TEARS AND SMILES.

A COMEDY.

IN FIVE ACTS.

PERFORMED AT THE THEATRE PHILADELPHIA.

BY J. N. BARKER.

FIRST ACTED WEDNESDAY, 4TH MARCH, 1807.

PHILADELPHIA,
PRINTED BY T. & G. PALMER,
FOR G. E. BLAKE, NO. 1, SOUTH THIRD-STREET.
....
1808.

PREFACE

A GOOD-NATURED friend of mine, to whom I submitted the manuscript of my play, before it was acted, after running his eyes over the pages, in a kind tone of voice requested me to throw it into the fire. Astonished and dismayed, I inquired the reason. " My dear sir," said my good-natured friend, " you are young; this is your maiden essay; and therefore I can pardon your inexperience. You meant to have written a comedy?" " I did." " And you have produced nothing, absolutely nothing but a collection of *Columbianisms*, in five parts." " And pray," asked I, " what may a Columbianism be?" " The term," replied my good-natured friend, " was invented and applied by certain hypercritics of our own, who, perhaps from being placed too near the scene, cannot discover the beauties of their own country, and whose refined taste is therefore better pleased with the mellow tints which distance gives to every foreign object. This term of derision they apply to every delineation an American may attempt to make of American manners, customs, opinions, characters, or scenery. Thus, while they rapturously applaud the sentiments of a foreign stage patriot, the lover of his country, in an American play, utters only contemptible Columbianisms. An allusion to the revolution which made us a nation, or to the inestimable characters who achieved it, cannot be heard with patience, though they may search history in vain for parallels to either. They can never pardon the endeavour to depict our national peculiarities, and yet they will listen with avidity to Yorkshire rusticity, or Newmarket slang. They can feel a poetic rapture, when some muddy stream of Europe flows in verse; but the author might as well incontinently drown himself in it, as lead the pastoral Schuylkill meandering through his poem. They can accompany the fop of an English play in his lounge through Bond-street, while an American personage, of the same cast, would most probably be knocked down, if he attempted a promenade in High-street. They find innumerable Columbianisms in language, too, in that city where all the world beside acknowledge the English tongue is spoken in its utmost purity. In fine, this unaccountable prejudice extends to every thing here; the farther, therefore, you remove from America, the nearer you approach to their favour. Take my advice, then; burn your book, write a melo-drame, and lay your scene in the moon."

When my d—d good-natured friend had finished, I took his advice precisely as advice is usually taken; that is, I didn't take it at all, but carried my play to the manager and had it acted. To say that I found the assertions of my good-natured friend entirely false, would be disingenuous; but not to clear a kind public from any the least share of reproach would be ungrateful. The play was received with, to say no more, all the polite and urbane toleration that the only sanguine friend I had, i.e., myself, could expect; and has been repeated oftener than once, without experiencing any diminution of public favour. But it was not difficult to discover the *anti*-Longinuses that my good-natured friend mentioned. They were as conspicuous as illiberality, ill nature, and ill manners could make them. While the benign Dispenser of light and life is thanked by the creature he makes happy, there are who even would propitiate evil deities, from whom they may fear harm. While I gratefully bend to a kind public, what shall I offer on the altars of hostile demons? Contempt: 'tis all I have. May the sacrifice be propitious!

PROLOGUE

Spoken by Mr. Wood

WITH swelling port, imperious and vain,
His war-horse pride, his coat of mail disdain,
Sir Prologue, like a knight of old romance,
Oft 'gainst puissant hosts has couch'd his lance;
While critic armies daring to the brunt,

He hurl'd his gauntlet at their marshal'd front.
Sometimes a different form the champion wears,
And lofty threat'nings leaves, for lowly prayers.
Then, crawling in the dust, with bated breath,
He vows your slightest frown were worse than death;
And haply lifts an axe, as whilom Bayes,
To chop his head off, if you fail to praise.
This Proteus greets ye undisguised to-night;
No Hector now, nor fawning parasite.
What think ye of his strange and bold design
Who cannot bully, and who will not whine?
A native of that soil where all are brave,
Shall he not spurn the language of a slave?
And here, where heartless judges ne'er appear,
Where mercy tempers justice, need he fear?
At ease then let us speak,—and, as the mode is,
In simile: to-night, our play a road is;
A stage-coach this same theatre shall be;
Which happ'ly throng'd with passengers I see,
Who crowded sit, bent on a small excursion,
To kill *ennui*, for health or for diversion.
Some wish the journey over ere begun;
Some pray for quiet slumbers, some for fun;
These hope the road is pleasant, but they doubt it;
Those swear 'tis bad, who nothing know about it.
Our Phaeton author mounts, with goose-quill whip,
And, smack! begins his first dramatic trip.
"The metaphor can never run," you cry,
"Sans horses!" Ah, sir! one of them am I!
Suppose, at length, all the five stages past,
And safe arriv'd our journey's end at last;
Good, gentle trav'lers, do not then, I pray,
Like some ungracious tourists, curse the way,
From Dan to Beersheba, and back to Dan,

As vile, simply because American.
But, if some humble beauties catch your sight,
Behold them in their proper, native light;
Not peering through discol'ring foreign prisms,
Find them but hideous, rank Columbianisms.
If in this path so little travell'd yet,
We meet nor accident, nor overset;
If our young Jehu take you smoothly through;
Nor rough you find the road, nor *enneuyeux;*
No lady rudely shock'd; no moral hurt;
Nor modesty nor virtue splash'd with dirt;
Say, will you—by those smiles I know you will—
Declare the youth displayed some little skill?
Nor fear, should chance e'er bring you the same way,
To trust yourselves with him some other day?

DRAMATIS PERSONÆ

General Campdon,	*Mr.* Warren,
Mr. Campdon,	Bray,
Osbert,	M'Kenzie,
Sydney,	Cain,
Rangely,	Wood,
Fluttermore,	Mills,
Monsieur Galliard,	Blissett,
O'Connor,	Robbins,
Nathan Yank,	Jefferson,
Servants,	*Messrs.* Durang *and* Seymour.
Madame Clermont,	*Mrs.* Melmoth,
Louisa Campdon,	Woodham,
Clara,	Jefferson,
Widow Freegrace,	Wood,
Miss Starchington,	Francis.

Scene—*In and near Philadelphia.* Time—12 *hours*

TEARS AND SMILES

Act I

Scene—*An apartment at Mr. Campdon's*

Enter General Campdon, *Mr.* Campdon

Camp. I must keep my promise, brother.

Gen. What! to barter your only daughter for certain lands and tenements? To sacrifice my niece to a puppy! a daffodil! who doesn't rank in merit with her lap-dog?

Camp. Handsome names these for an accomplished ward to receive from his guardian! Mr. Fluttermore is a fine gentleman, brother; a travelled gentleman.

Gen. A puppy! travelled with a vengeance! Yes; he leaves college a clever chubby-cheeked lad, with a florid hue in his countenance, and an honest love of country in his heart; and, after dropping his complexion and principle abroad, returns with a pale face, and a hearty contempt for every thing this side the water. Plague on it! when I suffered him to travel, I did not do my duty by the son of my old friend.

Camp. What! you would deny a young man of fortune the opportunity of acquiring a foreign polish and improvement?

Gen. Better so, brother, than to see him come home with nothing but the dirt of every soil he has walked over sticking to his feet. Improvement indeed! what has he gained? If I inquire of the present state of England, doesn't the pert fool entertain me with public breakfasts, private concerts, chalked floors, and pic-nic foolery? And but yesterday, when I wanted information of certain affairs of the continent, didn't he gravely give me the value of prince Eugene's wedding coat, and the altitude of his bride's feather?

Camp. Read the gazette, brother; read the gazette. You can't expect a gay young fellow to fill his head with a parcel of nonsense, merely to gratify your ridiculous passion for news.

Gen. "Nonsense!" "ridiculous passion!" your folly is intolerable; you should know, sir, that, as one of its members, our country is interested in every thing that takes place in the great family of nations. And as I have fought, brother, I can feel for its interests.

Camp. Ah! the old tale—you have fought. I confess I was always of a specific disposition, and preferred shedding ink to spilling blood; therefore, when you chose to be a soldier here in America, I was content with the character of a simple merchant at Hamburgh; and while I made an ample fortune in *my* pursuit, you lost in your's the little our father had left you.

Gen. I am proud of that circumstance.

Camp. Very like. Well, the country is now old enough to take care of itself; and the more fools they who trouble themselves about it, say I.

Gen. Go welcome the prisoners from the dungeons of Tripoli with that sentiment! Dry with it the tears that are shed for those who fell in attempting their deliverance, or generously give it in thanks to the brave survivors of *that* action which accomplished it!

Camp. How! have the prisoners returned? Then perhaps Sydney—

Gen. The noble boy has arrived also, with the proud consciousness of having shared in the glory of their liberation.

Camp. The devil! Sydney return'd! This is what I feared.

Gen. You are weary, then, of the orphan of your deceased friend? Well, sir, I'll take care of him; your avarice shall be gratified.

Camp. 'Sdeath, brother, how provoking is this! Hav'n't I, for I know not how long, cheerfully protected this orphan, and his sister too; and that without their having the least claim?

Gen. They have a strong claim on every man of feeling, for they are orphans; they have a particular claim on you, for they are the children of your friend.

Camp. Am I certain of that? What proof is there? Somewhere about eighteen years ago, an ugly, old withered Frenchman stalks into my counting-room at Hamburgh, with a pair of children in his hand, and a letter in his pocket; utters never a word, but leaving the letter and children, after kissing them all three, wipes his eyes, makes his *congé,* stalks out again, and is never heard of.

Gen. But the letter—

Camp. Ay, the letter. By some cursed accident, or more probably design, my correspondent's name is totally effaced; so that I remain ignorant what good-natured friend gets children for *me* to maintain. I shall always think it was the trick of some knave to palm his brats upon me; for I had no friend in France.

Gen. The extensive business you were then engaged in may have made you forgetful. The story the distressed writer told, could never have been feigned. Call to mind the pathetic terms in which he conjures you to be a father to his helpless children.

Camp. And I have been their father. Didn't I give them a family and name, because they had none of their own? Didn't I, in tenderness to their feelings, keep the whimsical mode of my becoming their patron a profound secret? Hav'n't I made them and the world believe they are children of my deceased friend Russel? Hav'n't I made them partakers of my fortune, and companions to my daughter?

Gen. You have.

Camp. Ay; and what's the return? Why, three years since, Heaven knows whither or for what, Miss Clara runs away; and Master Sydney seduces the affections of my daughter. And now, after sending him out of the way by getting him into the navy, here he returns.—But I'll prevent mischief. (*Rings the bell.*) She shall be married to-night, I am determined; and so I'll tell her.

Gen. But, brother—

Camp. Give me leave, sir; she's my daughter.

Gen. And therefore are you her tyrant?

Enter Servant

Camp. Tell Louisa I would speak with her.

Serv. Miss Campdon has gone out, sir.

Camp. Gone out?

Serv. Yes, sir, with Mrs. Freegrace.

Camp. Devil take Mrs. Freegrace! that confounded widow is the ruin of all daughters. (*To servant.*) Bring me my hat and stick. (*Exit servant.*) Perhaps she's this moment on her way to her beggarly paramour. I'll tramp the city, at any rate.

Gen. What folly is this?

Camp. I tell you, brother, if she gets a sight of the young dog in his blue uniform, it's all over with Fluttermore. The rascal's dirk will be more fatal to her filial duty than it ever was to his enemies; and even his cockade will have greater weight than my commands. I know these young jades. If she sees Sydney, she'll never have Fluttermore.

Gen. Then do I wish, with all my soul, that she may see him.

Camp. That's brotherly.

Enter Servant with hat and stick

Serv. Mr. O'Connor; to wait on you, sir. [*Exit.*

Gen. Now, brother, be advised; Mr. O'Connor will be proud of the commission; let him call for Louisa at the widow's, for I dare swear she's there; and you're so indiscreet, you'll make the affair ridiculous.

Camp. Well, but she shall be married to night. [*Exeunt.*

Scene—*The street*

Enter Widow Freegrace *and* Louisa

Lou. Pray let us return, my dear madam.

Wid. No; I'm determined to extend our walk. What, sit

moping at home this charming morning, listening to lectures on obedience from a father of threescore? Why, child, you'll so ruin your health, that Sydney will scarce know you for the same Louisa he left.

Lou. Ah, my dear madam, the return of Sydney, for which I have so often sighed, will only, I fear, hasten this detested marriage with Fluttermore to a completion.

Wid. And if ever you marry that wretch, I'll never forgive you.

Lou. How shall I avoid it?

Wid. E'en by running away with his rival; for if Sydney has the spirit I think he possesses, he'll propose the thing; and, unless you prefer a monkey to a man, you'll jump at the offer. But come; I promised Mrs. Clermont a how do ye this morning. You shall go with me.

Lou. You have frequently mentioned this lady's name, madam, but I have never heard from you precisely who she is.

Wid. That was, my dear, because I did not *precisely* know. During an eight years' acquaintance, I have learned that she is a foreigner confessedly; of condition most probably, from her elegant manners; and affluent certainly, from her style of living. Yet she sees very little company, and is scarcely known to any but those who need her assistance; while an air of dejection, which generally overspreads her fine features, seems to indicate that she has known misfortune. Altogether, she is one of the most interesting women I have ever seen.

Lou. Have you never inquired of her any particulars of her past life?

Wid. Never. There is a mild reserve about her, which constantly represses curiosity.

Lou. I am already disposed to love her.

Wid. And you shall love her; come—but, for heaven's sake no more sighing; for you shall have Sydney, in despite of that odious Fluttermore.

Lou. Ah, madam! I would you were a prophetess!

Wid. You shall find I am one, though I have to turn *sorceress* for it, and conjure him into the circle of your arms. Come. *Esperance!* my dear girl. [*Exeunt.*

Scene—*An apartment in a hotel*

Rangely, *finishing his toilet*

There, Jack Rangely, I think you're decent enough now for a stroll. A stroll; and will you ever be a stroller, Jack? You're absolutely an itinerant rake by profession; and you do follow your business most industriously, in every town of the union, that's the truth of it. But will you never change your character to that of a good orderly kind of a—oh! yes; could I meet with that enchanting creature that fortune threw into my way, merely, I believe, to have the pleasure of taking away again, she might transform me in a twinkling: but I don't know her name; nay, she may be married. No matter; she's in this city, and I *will* find her. (*Looks at his watch.*) Gad! the morning flies; here have I been a whole night, and half a day, in Philadelphia, without stirring a foot in search. Where can this Yank loiter?

Enter Nathan Yank, *hastily*

Yank. Beg pardon, sir, for being out o' the way, and out o' breath. Hope you ha'n't wanted—whew.

Ran. How now, Yank! why man, you've lost your breath.

Yank. Not quite, sir; though an *'twer* gone for good, I should be 'nation glad to lose it for you, sir; ay, and what's more nor that, my life into the bargain.

Ran. Pshaw! remember what I've told you.

Yank. And mayn't I remember what you've done for me too, sir? How you found me and old folks sick, and nothing to eat but pumpkins; and how you put old folks into a tidy house, and gave 'em money; and made me your man? I reckon I can't forget it, sir.

Ran. You know I hate to hear this.

Yank. Mortal sorry for that, sir, 'cause I do like to talk about it. It makes me to feel so 'tarnal queer and good, all over about like.

Ran. How have you spent your morning, Yank?

Yank. I'll discount my adventers, sir. First and foremost I looked if your baggage wer safe and sound; afterward, I saw horses had a belly-full, and then I ate my breakfast. Secondly, I made black Will wash curricle, grease wheels, and so; and then I basted Frenchified gentlemen's servant for calling me Yankey Doodle.

Ran. What Frenchified gentlemen?

Yank. Only two *mounsheers*, that live in this here house. Well, ater I lick'd servant, I run to buy some *imperious* wash for your boots, and who do you count I seed go in a door?

Ran. Nay, how should I know?

Yank. But only guess.

Ran. Blockhead! I can't guess.

Yank. Why, lord, sir, don't you mind that 'ere beautiful lady that wer jest goin to break her beautiful neck, 'cause her horses wou'dn't stop, near York, you know, when you spoilt your best coat, 'cause when you jumpt out o' curricle so quick to lay hold on 'em, you tumbled in the mud?

Ran. Heavens! my incognita! are you sure 'twas she?

Yank. I don't know her name's Cognita, but I'm sure 'twer she. I took notice enough that time when you were so long with her: for I had nought to do, not I, but look on and whistle.

Ran. Well; you saw her, you say—

Yank. Go into a door.

Ran. Lead me instantly to the spot. You know the house?

Yank. Lord, sir, I clean forgot to take notice.

Ran. Idiot!

Yank. Yes, sir, I know you allow me none o' the 'cutest, but may be I could find out.

Ran. On then, good Yank, and task your ingenuity.

Yank. Yes, sir. Let me see; first, there wer a church; and then—

Ran. Away, my fine fellow, away! [*Exeunt.*

Scene—*The street*

Enter O'Connor

What a fool's errand am I sent on! Devil a Miss Louisa can I see at the widow's, nor no part of the charming widow herself either, except the ugly old maid, her sister. So, finding the bird flown, and the empty cage, with nothing at all but a tabby in it, I made bold to fly too; for I believe the old mouser has a design upon my own person. 'Pon my faith, though, I wish I had met with the widow. Och! but these females do boder us Irish gentlemen, to be sure. When my head was no higher than my knee, little Judy threw her sparklers upon me, and made something leap in my breast like a salmon. And, since then, to the music of how many pairs of eyes has my heart capered? Let me see.

Song

Fair Jane
First beat a rub-a dub
With her two eyes; oh! she drumm'd on the heart o' me;
Mary M'Shane
Then made a hub-a bub,
Piping her's prettily when forced to part from me;
Next the keys of my bosom touch'd Katy O'Fogarty;
But soon a sad part
Was play'd on my heart,
For its strings were all snapt by the cruel Miss Dougherty
What a crash!
All to smash
Went every part o' me.
Oh, fie!
Cruel Miss Dougherty,
How could you handle so roughly the heart o' me?

Poor soul!
I sail'd o'er the ocean now
Sighing, heart broken, and loving the moon and night.
Heart whole!
'Tis always in motion now;
Jumping so merrily, morning and noon and night.
In this land of beauty, each sparkling eye shedding bright
Joy with each glance,
Bids the heart nimbly dance;
And och, widow! how my heart will jig on our wedding night.
Dancing still,
Prancing still,
Morning and noon and night,
O Love!
Give me my widow, do;
Let me again sigh and wish for the moon and night.

[*Exit.*

Enter Rangely *and* Yank

Yank. I'll be darned, sir, if I think this is the way, for I can't see a morsel of a church. If I could only once spy out the church.

Ran. A plague upon your pilotship, you stupid—Hey! what sparks have we here?

Yank. Never budge, if they arn't the Frenchified folks!

Ran. I think I should know that face: it is Fluttermore. But his dress! What a metamorphosis!

Enter Fluttermore *and* Galliard

Ned! my dear Ned!

Flut. Ned! (*Sees Rangely.*) ha! Jack Rangely, by gad!

Ran. Honest Ned, I'm so glad to see you—

[*Shakes his hand cordially.*

Flut. That you mean to dislocate my shoulder. Hold, for heav'n's sake! or you'll shake my whole system into *derangement;* the bones out of my body, and the powder out of my head!

Ran. (*Examining his figure.*) But what the devil!

Flut. Ay, you wonder, Jack. A little *transformé,* you see.

Ran. You are indeed.

Flut. Yes, burst from darkness into the blaze of fashion; chang'd in an instant—

Ran. From a worm to a butterfly.

Flut. Butterfly! yes, faith; good metaphor. Once a book-worm, a college chrysalis; now a butterfly, light, airy, *emerillоné.* 'Gad, a *bonne similitude*—Made the grand tour.

Ran. The grand tour?

Flut. Yes; just returned. Hey, monsieur? 'Gad, I beg pardon. This sudden *rencontre* with my friend—Give me leave —This is *monsieur Galliard,* from Paris. Monsieur, my friend, Jack Rangely, from—no matter. There; don't shake hands: that's antique. Talk English, Jack; Galliard prefers it; speaks it like a native.

Gal. Oh! lit, ver lit; *presque rien;* noting 'tall.

Flut. No; believe me, he swears English with the best accent.

Gal. Oh! I'll be dam! You flatte me.

Flut. Judge!

Ran. And what do you think, M. Galliard, of North America and its savages?

Gal. *Comment?* Sauvage! As I hope to be save, I have not seen—

Ran. I mean its inhabitants: for doubtless we must appear uncivilized to you polished Europeans.

Gal. Your good pardon, sare; *c'est un bon pay;* ver good fine contrée; *tous les hommes,* all de peuple happy; all de vomen belle, beautiful! By gar, I am ravish'd!

Ran. You praise lavishly, M. Galliard.

Flut. He does, indeed. For my part, I can't conceive what you possibly do in this corner of the globe. No opera; no masquerade, nor *fete,* nor *conversazione;* a diabolical theatre; and not even a *promenade,* where one might—(*Examining his figure.*) Then your women; such dowdies! No air; no manner. And your men: *O Ciel!* such beings!—'Gad, Jack, you must go to Europe! You see what it can do.

Ran. Why, if I could hope ever to attain that brilliancy—

Flut. Pshaw, man! don't despair. There are very pretty degrees, you know, below the *summit* of excellence. I rather fancy, indeed, that the *eclat* which attended *me* is not to be repeated every day. Why, sir, I was absolutely a comet.

Ran. Indeed!

Flut. Set Paris in a blaze; shook London to its centre; dazzled most of the Italian cities; made Vienna totter; and was the gaze every where. Ha, monsieur?

Gal. *Oh! oui;* wherever you are, *de peuple gape at you.* Yes; dam 'tis not true.

Flut. Then for the women. I don't know what can be found so delectable about me; but in strict truth, all ranks—Hark ye, Jack: *entre nous*—

[*Whispers.*

Ran. The princess! Impossible!

Flut. True; poor Eugene! As to the wives and daughters of petty princes or electors; pretty *amusettes,* or so, for an idle hour. Show you my diary.

Ran. What, did you keep a diary?

Flut. Not a vulgar gazetteer-like thing; distance of post-towns, and all that—*Le voici!*

[*Shows a small morocco book.*

Ran. Heavens! here's a list of names might become the docket of a sheriff of the county!

Flut. A few. This side, princes, or so, my particular friends, with whom I've passed whole *days.* *L'autre coté,* princesses, and that kind of thing, with whom I've pass'd whole—(*ahem*)—hey, monsieur?

Gal. Oh, *by de lor,* you have good mode *pour passer le temps.* Yes.

Ran. Excellent pastime, I dare swear. But have you gained nothing else? No observations, remarks?

Flut. Oh! customs and manners, and all that; laws, and the like. O yes; profound too. The English can't dress, talk, nor cook so well as the French. The Italian opera is a dev'lish deal finer than any thing in the world. The *elegantes* have introduced hair-powder into Paris; and the emperor, gun-powder into Germany. Then for laws; for laws. They are every where better than *ours,* because every where else the *bourgeois* are kept under. *En fin,* I have found that the new world is too green to please the palate of a man of *gusto;* and that Europe, like a ripe beauty, is the only object worthy a connoisseur's attention.

Gal. *Eh bien!* For me, I tink Europe is like de old libertine, de courtesane; I am disgust vid her. Amerique is de lit demoiselle you point me in de street; vat you call?

Flut. Ha! ha! A Quaker!

Gal. Ah! de quake; yes. So *ingenue,* so *modest:* as I hope to be save, I vill choose de *contrée* and de quake for life. I vill marry de *one,* and settle in de *oder.*

Flut. Oh! desist, Galliard, in pity. Ha! ha!

Gal. Yes; I ave made my mind. I will marry de lit quake gal. Dam 'tis not true.

Flut. Ha! ha! But, Jack, I havn't inquired into your affairs yet. What are you at? What's your present pursuit?

Ran. A woman!

Flut. I thought so. You keep your old tricks of the college.

Ran. No, 'faith! this is an honourable pursuit. I had the happiness to save a charming woman from some danger, occasioned by a fright her horses had taken. Such an angel! with a vivacity so enchanting! a mind so cultivated! a voice so musical! Oh! Ned, had you heard her thank me! Then, her eyes, her lips—

Flut. Her nose, her chin; proceed in your inventory. Gad, the fellow's mad! The woman has bewitched you, Jack.

Ran. True; she did bewitch me; for though the accident furnished me with an opportunity for a delightful tete-a-tete, curse me if I think I uttered twenty syllables in the time. I am induced to believe I did exercise the gallantry of handing her into her carriage though; for, when I awoke from the spell, I found myself a senseless clod in the midst of the road, my angel out of sight, and I unacquainted with her name, and profoundly ignorant whether she was maid, wife, or widow.

Flut. Oh! poor Jack! ha! ha! ha!

Gal. *En vérité, 'tis von comical avanture. Mais* it is happy de carriage not run ovare you too, like de oder clod; ah, ha!

Yank. I took care o' that, sir: I gove him a pull.

Flut. Who the devil—

Ran. My man Nathan, gentlemen; a very honest fellow.

Flut. A wise man of the east, I perceive. But, apropos to women, Jack: I'll introduce you to my *shall-be* wife.

Ran. Are you serious?

Flut. As a preacher. I've prevailed on myself at last. Louisa is *là là;* isn't she, Galliard? But wants forming. Marry her for that; model her myself. You shall see her today; my worshipful guardian has invited me to his villa to dine. You shall go. No resistance; you shall.

[*Walk apart.*

Enter Widow Freegrace *and* Louisa

Wid. Fr. You have made no contemptible conquest, my dear. Mrs. Clermont is not pleased with every one thus.

Lou. Oh Heaven! there's that hateful lover of mine!

Wid. Fr. And my dumb deliverer, as I am a widow.

Lou. Let us avoid him, madam.

Wid. Fr. We can't, child. Drop your veil; his eyes are not penetrative enough to discover you.

Lou. But he'll know you.

Wid. Fr. Mine shall down too; so. But my spark shall see me, I'm resolved.

Yank. (*To Rangely.*) That's she, sir.

Rang. Which? Who?

Yank. Cognita.

As they pass over, Widow Freegrace lifts up a part of her veil

Ran. 'Tis she, by Heaven!

Wid. Fr. He'll answer the challenge; certainly.

[*Exeunt Widow Freegrace and Louisa.*

Ran. I can't be mistaken. Adieu, gentlemen.

[*Going.*

Flut. Adieu! Why, where are you going?

Ran. We're at the same hotel: I'll meet ye there.

Flut. We'll walk there together, if you please.

[*Taking his arm.*

Ran. Excuse me, I have business.

Flut. Defer it. Help yourself to the other pinion, monsieur.

Gal. Oui, or de bird vill fly. Yes—ah, ha!

Ran. This is rudeness—

Flut. You are rude, to attempt running away thus.

Ran. Well; release me. I will not leave ye.

Flut. Honour!

Ran. Honour!

Flut. Release him, Galliard.

Gal. Oui, yes—de string of honare vill hold de bird. Yes—

Ran. (*To Yank.*) Follow, and observe closely where she goes; don't fail for your life. (*Exit Yank.*) Gentlemen, perhaps the idea don't happen to occur to ye, that you have spoiled an affair that—

Flut. Oh, no! we see the affair. Ha! Galliard?

Gal. Ay! O yes! ve behold vat de bird would fly at; ah, ha!

Flut. Pshaw! Rangely, don't pout, you shall be a gainer by this. When I get you in Europe, I'll remunerate you with a dozen duchesses.

Ran. Curse the coxcomb! at such a time—

Flut. Come, gloomy, 'tis time to dress—on to the hotel.

Gal. *Allons donc.* [*Exeunt.*

Act II

Scene—*At Mr. Campdon's*

Campdon *enters, followed by* O'Connor

O'Con. I suppose the young lady's taking a little bit of a walk, just.

Camp. Walk! I tell you she's taking a bit of a gallop: by this time half way to Washington. And that infernal widow has lent her carriage for the purpose. I see it.

O'Con. Infernal widow! O fie! it's mighty ungentale of you. You know I'm that lady's lover, sir.

Camp. Oh, hang her. John! [*Calling.*

O'Con. Hang yourself, you ugly old gentleman!

Camp. John, are the horses put to?

Enter Louisa *and Widow* Freegrace

Lou. Horses! why, sir, are you going so early to my uncle's?

Camp. So; you're forced to return; ha? What! was your carriage broken, your nags lame, madam? Why didn't you scamper off, minx?

Wid. Fr. Now what does the silly man mean?

Lou. I hope my father does not suspect—

Camp. But your father does suspect. Didn't that baggage Clara run away? And wouldn't you, if you could? I know your sex, and you're all runagates, devils.

Wid. Fr. Did you ever hear? Am I a devil, Mr. O'Connor?

O'Con. An angel, madam, or I'm no true believer. O! for shame, Mr. Campdon, to speak so of the ladies. Sweet creatures! what would the world be without them?

Camp. Peaceable, at least. Confound them for a parcel of plagues!

O'Con. Plagues!

Camp. Ay, a daughter's a positive plague; a wife's a worse; and a widow's the torment superlative. There's grammar for you.

Wid. Fr. Ha! ha! But why, Mr. Campdon, are you in such haste to marry Louisa, and thus, according to your rules, make her the second degree of bad—a wife?

Camp. Simply to get rid of the first, a daughter; and at present I wish I was fairly rid of the last.

Wid. Fr. A widow! a palpable hit! Certainly, my dear, your father has the pleasantest way with him, the most facetious mode of turning one out of doors.

Lou. Nay, do not think any thing my father says—

Camp. Worth attending to—is that it, miss pert?

Wid Fr. O, child, 'tis a charming morning recreation. If he'd set chairs, I would chat an hour with him in this sociable way.

Camp. I'll not be laughed at in my own house; and let me tell you, madam—

Wid. Fr. Keep your distance; I won't box with you, that's flat: nay, don't burst with passion, I'm going; I pass the day with Mrs. Clermont. Louisa, I'll drop in this evening and bring her with me.

Camp. And who is Mrs. Clermont?

Wid. Fr. A widow, don Curiozo.

Camp. I'll have no more widows; I hate widows.

O'Con. Upon my conscience, that's what I call very strange.

Lou. My dear sir, Mrs. Clermont is one of the best of women.

Camp. Bad is the best. A counterpart of this, I dare say.

Wid. Fr. No, poor thing. As unlike me as possible.

Camp. Then there's some hope that she's tolerable.

Wid. Fr. Civil creature! Come, sir knight, deliver me from this enchanted castle. Adieu, Merlin.

[*Exeunt O'Con. and Widow.*

Camp. Thank heaven that pestilence is gone. And now,

miss, a word with you. I have fixed my mind on having your marriage take place tonight.

Lou. Tonight! you can't mean it: consider, my dear father—

Camp. I have considered, my dear daughter, that if Fluttermore don't get you tonight, Sydney may to morrow. So prepare for the solemnities. [*Going.*

Lou. I cannot marry Fluttermore, sir.

Camp. How! What?

Lou. Not so suddenly. Let me have a little time to—to think; to—

Camp. To form plots? Think, indeed! you've thought too much of that *viper* that I have nourished.

Lou. Sir, had I never seen Sydney, my aversion to Fluttermore would still be equal to what it is.

Camp. Aversion! These novel-reading misses! And pray what the devil gives you this *aversion*, as you call it?

Lou. An assemblage of every thing disagreeable. Is he not a frivolous coxcomb?

Camp. Hum! A little so. But his estate—

Lou. Besides, he's a libertine.

Camp. No.

Lou. Not a libertine?

Camp. No, I tell you. To be sure the young man does talk of this and of that; but, I dare engage, he's quite a harmless, innocent kind of a gentleman.

Lou. Then the stories he is continually relating.

Camp. All bounce; not a word true.

Lou. How contemptible!

Camp. How agreeable! you mean. Why he'll be the most diverting husband! a fanciful amour of his, told over a dish of chocolate, will so amuse ye! For, you know, you need'nt care to be angry, when you know it isn't true. You'll have a living *romance* for life, child, so inexhaustible that you need never again apply to a circulating library.

Lou. But, sir, as I have no relish at present for this gay humour of his, give me a short time to grow familiar with it?

Camp. Pshaw! You'll grow familiar enough, and get a relish too, when you're married.

Lou. Give me one month?

Camp. To night, when you return from your uncle's.

Lou. A week, sir! Respite me for a single day?

Camp. To night! I'm determined. [*Exit.*

Lou. Say you so? Then I am determined too, and this tyranny warrants the resolution which my heart had formed. [*Exit.*

Scene—*An apartment at Mrs. Clermont's*

Mrs. Clermont *discovered reading*

Mrs. C. (*Throwing the book by.*) Alas! how vain is this philosophy! And how inefficient the lapse of years to lull the disturbed mind to rest! The mere *remembrance* of what was, arises, and, by its powerful breath, the illusory calm becomes a tempest! Oh heaven! let me forget that I was once so blest! Hope has long since died! let memory too expire!

Enter a Servant

Ser. Miss Starchington, madam, is on the stairs.

Mrs. C. Show her in here; I will wait on her immediately. (*Exit Servt.*) These foolish tears! [*Exit.*

Enter Miss Starchington *and Servant*

Miss S. Didn't you say your mistress was here?

Ser. She will wait on you instantly, madam. [*Exit.*

Miss S. Well, of all things in the world, I do want to discover *who* and *what* this Mrs. Clermont is. I don't like to be suspicious; and yet, if I were so disposed, such splendour, and such mystery! To be sure, she's not handsome; but then there's no accounting for men's tastes; their neglect of me prove that. The mischief is, no men visit her; that is, not publicly. I'm sure I am neither curious nor suspicious, but I must find her out; for though my sister Freegrace almost adores her, I don't think she's any better than she—

Enter Mrs. Clermont

My dear Mrs. Clermont, how d'ye do? I declare you look charming this morning; quite a roseate bloom.

Mrs. C. You have more good nature than my glass, Miss Starchington.

Miss S. But not quite so much sincerity. [*Apart.*

Mrs. C. If nothing else had blanched my cheek, too many winters have passed over it to leave any trace of the rose there.

Miss S. I meant the white rose. (*Apart.*) Certainly, my dear madam, nothing, as you say, is so terrible a bleacher of the skin as sorrow.

Mrs. C. Did *I* say sorrow?

Miss S. It makes shocking havock.

Mrs. C. That cannot be doubted.

Miss S. Especially when it proceeds from one's own imprudence, or the misfortune of losing one's reputation! and, in that case, what's the use of ever so much riches? I wouldn't wonder if people's cheeks were pale *then.* My reputation is every thing to me, and indeed so is the reputation of my friends; and for that reason, Mrs. Clermont, I take your part so.

Mrs. C. My part?

Miss S. Yes: when the impertinent world asks a thousand foolish questions about you; such as, Who is this Mrs. Clermont? Where did she come from? What means has she? Is she a widow, or a wife, or a—I answer immediately, why, Lord bless you, I dare say Mrs. Clermont is neither ashamed nor afraid to tell all about the matter, says I, if I ask her.

Mrs. C. And does this satisfy the world?

Miss S. Not quite: and indeed, my dear madam, I wish I did know a little more of your affairs.

Mrs. C. I'm truly sorry that my affairs should give *you* any trouble, my *good friend.*

Miss S. Oh! madam, it would be the greatest pleasure— Pshaw! my sister; how provoking!

Enter Widow Freegrace *and* O'Connor

Mrs. C. This quick return is kind.

Wid. Fr. I am welcome somewhere then! Ah, sister—

Mrs. C. Can there be that place on earth where you are not welcome?

Wid. Fr. Heavens! why there are some people who would as lief see Starchington as me: are you to learn, that I am charged with spoiling all the young girls, I know? Isn't it so, Starchington?

Miss S. Why, indeed, you do encourage the forward chits too much, sister Freegrace.

Wid. Fr. There! my own flesh and blood. But this morning I've had it roundly from little Louisa's father. Had he had his militia sword in his hand, I should have trembled for my life; that is, if O'Connor hadn't stood between us.

O'Con. Ah! madam, if the old gentleman had made the attack, I would have been but a poor safeguard.

Wid. Fr. Indeed!

O'Con. Yes: for his sword would have found you in *my* heart as soon as in your own.

Wid. Fr. That compliment comes from the heart, however.

Miss S. Mr. O'Connor will say his civil thing, though he labour ever so much for it.

O'Con. Not always. To some people I wouldn't put myself to any trouble about the matter.

Mrs. C. But can nothing prevent this marriage, so utterly disagreeable to Miss Campdon?

Wid. Fr. I fear nothing; unless she takes my sage counsel and runs away.

Miss S. There, sister! these are your notions of propriety. For my part, I wonder what the romantic thing would have. To be sure, Fluttermore is a coxcomb; but he's better than the fellow she would throw herself away upon.

O'Con. Upon my honour and credit, Sydney is a fine fellow, and deserves her.

Wid. Fr. And shall have her.

Mrs. C. If his humble situation be his only want of merit, he may deserve an empress.

Miss S. Sister, pray favour me with your sal volatile: the air of this apartment is absolutely so confined—

Mrs. C. Permit me to conduct you to the drawing-room; 'tis more open and agreeable.

Wid. Fr. We follow you. [*Exeunt.*

Scene—*The street before Mrs. Clermont's house*

Enter Rangely *and* Yank

Ran. Come on, Yank; gad, I believe I've given them the slip.

Yank. Yes, sir; only I hope the horses won't give us the slip, and run away with the curricle that you left at the door.

Ran. You're sure you are right now, Yank?

Yank. Sartain, sir: you see ater I tracked her to a house, I waited awhile at the door, and bye and bye out comes she, but ony with a man, not the other lady that were with her.

Ran. With a man did you say? A young man?

Yank. Middling.

Ran. The devil!

Yank. Naught like him, sir—purtyish enough, like me or you.

Ran. Well!

Yank. So, sir, ater she kept dodging about, here and there, like a Jack-a-lantern; at last, when she went into this house here, thinking she mought be minded to rest a morsel, I run to tell you, sir.

Ran. And where's the house?

Yank. Stay a bit; do ye see yan church?

Ran. Well! she don't live in a church?

Yank. Ony o' Sundays, sir. Wait; there's the church; well, one two, three—

Ran. What are you at?

Yank. Four, five, six. There, sir; you allowed I had'n't no gumption. That's the house, sir.

Ran. That?

Yank. That very 'dentical one, sir.

Ran. Then here lives my angel! But stop! I don't know her name; what excuse—

Enter Fluttermore *and* Galliard

Flut. We'll save you the trouble of inventing one.

Yank. Oh Lord! here's the comet again!

Ran. Confusion!

Gal. A ha! mons. Jack; ve ave tumble upon you!

Flut. Hey! why you wouldn't enter that house?

Ran. And why not that house?

Flut. *Seulement* this. If you have no usher but Impudence, your reception won't be the most flattering in the universe.

Ran. What do you mean?

Flut. Simply, that the lady of that house, with age enough to be *your* mama, has sufficient dignity for that of *Napoleon le grand*, and with high blood to feel an insult, has sturdy servants to turn the impudent rake who offers it out of doors.

Ran. You're jesting.

Flut. Ask Galliard.

Gal. *Certainement*, yes; madame Clermont 'as great much de *hauteur*, by de lor!

Flut. Here comes my noble guardy; you'll believe a general, I hope.

Enter General Campdon

General, give me leave—a particular friend of mine, Jack Rangely; Jack, my guardian, General Campdon.

Gen. What! son of Jack Rangely of Virginia?

Ran. At your command, sir.

Gen. I knew your father, sir: a worthy man, and an able officer; one who loved his country and his friend well enough to lose his life for either. Sir, I am happy to meet you. [*Rangely bows.*]

Flut. We want your assistance at council, General. Rangely here, unlike his father, chuses the field of *love* to show his prowess in; and because, in his campaigns, he has overcome certain petty fortresses, fancies he can subdue the old gallic citadel within the walls here; he had sat down, in form, before it, and was actually proceeding to the storm when I entered. How say you, sir, will he succeed?

Gen. Is he serious, Mr. Rangely, for I never know when to have him?

Ran. My friend, sir, takes the liberty of jesting, at times.

Gal. Oui, Mr. Fluttermore love *de badinage infinement;* yes.

Ran. So far from having any design on the lady he describes, upon my soul! I never saw her.

Flut. Then what the deuce were you going in there for? I can safely swear there is no other female there above the dignified rank of a chambermaid.

Ran. (*To Yank.*) You have made some confounded mistake here.

Yank. No, sir; sartain I seed young cognita go in yan. Old gallic cittydale, indeed! It were no sich a body.

Flut. But apropos! if I recollect right, gad! I believe I'm to be married to night—didn't you say something of that kind?

Gen. Was there ever such a lukewarm—

Flut. Why, lord! would you have me get into a passion about a bagatelle?

Gen. Bagatelle, sir! have you no sensibility of your happiness, in getting the finest girl in the world?

Flut. O lord! yes, a vast deal of sensi—but as to raptures and extacies, and that kind of thing, gad they're all out; left the fashionable world long since. Those monopolizers, the novelists, have bought up all the old-fashioned article, and if you want it now, you must apply to the only shop where 'tis to be had; *savoir,* the circulating library.

Gal. Stop lit, monsieur, *vous oubliez,* you forget *en Europe* de princess, de lit *amusette* or so.

Flut. True, monsieur, true; egad I did bring the antique thing a little *en mode,* I can't deny it: the women did love me, *en peu, a' la romance.*

Gen. Oh god of foppery! had you ever such a votary.

Ran. I can't envy your feelings, Ned, simply, because you have none: but were I so fortunate! had I my unknown!—

Gal. And me too besides: suppose I had my lit quake.

Flut. *O Dieu!* here I stand, like the wall that parted Pyramus and Thisbe, doom'd to hear sighs and wishes on both sides: "my Thisbe dear!" ha! ha!

Gen. One consolation, I have done every thing in my power to prevent a lovely young creature's being tied to you for life, Mr. *wall!*

Flut. I acknowledge your kind guardianship in every particular, my dear General.

Gen. Would that guardianship were over, my dear brick-and-mortar.

Flut. Nay, we won't quarrel; men of mode never quarrel—Isn't it time to ride, guardy? I've taken the liberty to invite Mr. Rangely—

Gen. For once, your liberty is not impertinent. Mr. Rangely, you will do me honour. (*Rangely bows.*) Come, shall we set out?

Flut. (*Takes Rangely's arm.*) You shan't escape this time.

Ran. 'Tis vain to strive—my cursed fortune! have with ye, gentlemen.

Nods significantly to Yank, and exit with them

Yank remains; Mrs. Freegrace *appears at the window*

Wid. Fr. 'Twas certainly he, and with General Campdon.

Yank. (*Imitating Rangely's nod.*) Now, whether that should signify Yank stay here, or Yank follow ater, darn me if I can tell.

Wid. Fr. I wish I were sure he was seeking me: hang him, I'm getting too much interested.

Yank. I'll argufy the tropic, as the man says in the show—Well, if I stay here, he gallops out o' town, and I can't find *him;* and if I go away, why she may trot out o' the house, and so I lose *her*.

Wid. Fr. As I live, his servant!

Yank. I never wer at sich a stand. (*The door opens.*) Here's somebody comin; never budge but I'll gist ask about the matter: I must go cute about it, though.

O'Connor *comes from the house*

O'Con. 'Tis time to attend to my engagement. I must e'en canter to General Campdon's; and yet, by the powers, I am sorry to leave my sweet widow.

Yank (*Approaching ridiculously.*) Sarvant, sir. Pray, sir—hem! As you come out o' yan house, you mought tell a body—Pray, sir—hem! What o'clock mought it be, sir?

O'Con. A strange fellow! Because I come out of that house!—'Tis two o'clock, my lad. [*Going.*

Yank. Thank ye, sir; much obligated to you, sir; and mought I be so bold as to put another question to you, sir? Pray, does old Gallic Cittydale, or young Cognita live in yan?

O'Con. Now what are you talking about?

Yank. You don't know?

O'Con. Get away, you big blockhead.

Yank. I saw you fetching a walk with Miss Cognita, sir.

O'Con. You're mad. I know no such person. Well, now for Campdon's villa. [*Exit.*

Yank. Big blockhead! I wonder who's the biggest! He comes pop out of a house, and don't know who lives in it. Then he fetches a walk with Miss Cognita, and don't know no sitch a person; and now he's going to canter to Campdon's willow. Campdon's! 'Cod; the very place! I'll follow him to my master, at a venter. [*Going.*

Wid. Fr. To my wish: his servant inquiring for me. Yank!

Yank. Lord! who knows me? Ma'am!—ha—no—yes—it is, by jing? How d'ye do, ma'am? I thought I couldn't be mistaken. I'm so glad. Good bye, ma'am.

Wid. Fr. Stop! whither are you hurrying.

Yank. To general Thingumbob's, ma'am, to tell him the news. Only tell me one thing: is your name Gallic Cittydale?

Wid. Fr. No; my name is—

Yank. Cognita. Yes, that's what he calls you. Good bye, ma'am.

Wid. Fr. But stay!

Yank. Yes, ma'am, he'll be out of his wits for joy; and *he*'ll be out of sight: and I don't know my way. Good bye, ma'am. I'll tell him the truth. Cittydale, indeed! Good bye, ma'am. [*Exit.*

Wid. Fr. Plague take the stupid fellow! However, Rangely is with the Campdons, and we shall soon meet, certainly. [*Closes the window.*

Act III

Scene—*The street*

Enter Osbert *and* Sydney

Osb. For shame! restrain this fretful impatience. You have learned, you say, that she will return to town this evening?

Syd. Yes, she will return; but it will be as the bride of my rival. When I left you, Mr. Osbert, to seek Louisa, my bosom was light. Absence had made me forget the disparity of our fortunes; and, elated beyond myself, I indulged the hope—But to find her on the very eve of this detested marriage! To night, the servants said: nay, perhaps this moment the ceremony is performing; perhaps already done. Oh, madness!

Osb. Madness, indeed! Be calm, Sydney, be calm.

Syd. Let grey philosophy be calm; 'tis the privilege of youth to speak what nature prompts.

Osb. Rather say, 'tis the privilege of a lover to rave.

Syd. Even so; while the cold pedant stands by, and wonders that a man can feel. You may be calm, Mr. Osbert, for love raises no storm in your bosom; you may preach patience to a phrenzied mind, and think to succeed, for you know not what it is to love and to despair.

Osb. This is the very petulant boast of every vain sufferer, who fancies his own light ills outweigh the miseries of the world beside; and, while he feels the thorn pierce his own breast, forgets that one more deadly may rankle in the bosom of another. Love and despair! Sydney, I *have* known them. I was young once; was happy. For a few fleeting moments Love entwined his roseate arms around me. Sydney, for twenty years have I hugged despair!

Syd. Sir, your words! your manner!—

Osb. You thought me cold, unfeeling. Young man, did you know my story—

Syd. You interest me strongly. Pray, impart it.

Osb. I will: for it may furnish you with a useful lesson. Listen, then. I became at an early age an orphan. Entirely unconnected with the world and impelled by a youthful passion for travel, I disposed of my slender patrimony, and landed in Europe. It was in the south of France, I first saw—

[*Becomes affected.*

Syd. Nay, sir—

Osb. One tear to her memory! The richest boon that Heaven has in its gift was mine: the heart of a lovely and virtuous woman. We loved with all the ardour of youth; our souls were indissolubly knit together. But my Adelaide was heiress of a noble house, and her proud family disdained a presumptuous plebeian's alliance. We, in our turn, despising the paltry considerations of rank, and giddy with passion, sought for happiness in a clandestine marriage.

Syd. And did not felicity follow?

Osb. Misery. Listen! By the perfidy of a confidant, our secret was developed ere we could leave France; my Adelaide, torn from my arms, was hurried to a convent, and lost to me for ever.

Syd. Alas! and yourself?

Osb. After a confinement of some time in the chateau, I was bid to fly from the vengeance of an injured family, with two lovely infants, the offspring of what they termed our guilt; and in giving which to the world, they told me, my Adelaide had died. But when, distrustful of this story, I still lingered near the convent, I was seized by my implacable foes, and rudely conveyed to Toulon, whence a vessel was to take me, I know not whither; for, the day after sailing, she became the prize of a barbarian pirate.

Syd. O Heaven! But your children?

Osb. Happily, they were left in the care of a faithful servant, to whom I found means to write, instructing him to place them under the protection of a dear friend in Germany.

Syd. How fortunate! And do they live?

Osb. Alas! after thirteen years of slavery, I effected my escape, and flew to the birth-place of my wife; but the flames of the revolution had reached it; the convent that had confined her was demolished; the noble seat of her ancestors was in ruins, and her haughty family extinct for ever! I sought my children in Germany; but my friend had long before disappeared, or perhaps died, and was forgotten. Then it was I felt myself a solitary, unloved, and unregarded wretch; for, till our friendship commenced so romantically at Gibraltar, Sydney, in the wide world there lived not one whose hand, when I grasped it, would return the pressure of kindness. Tell me, then, think ye I have not known despair?

Syd. Oh, sir, forgive my culpable rashness!

Osb. My young friend, I have given this tedious lecture only that you might derive a comfort from the contrast of our miseries. Mark then the vast difference, and be happy.

Syd. Happy! Oh no! the fantastic visions of my boyish fancy have given place to a gloomy reality. Like *you*, sir, I court an alliance with those who—

Osb. You have already told me. Your Louisa's family is rich?

Syd. To abundance.

Osb. And yourself poor?

Syd. As my worst enemy could wish. But yet you do not know me, for when I told you I was poor, an absurd pride forbad me to add dependent; dependent, too, on the bounty of *her* father; and shall I—oh folly! shall the needy orphan Russel dare to hope for Louisa Campdon!

Osb. Campdon?

Syd. Campdon. Did I never repeat the name before?

Osb. Never! Campdon!

Syd. That's extraordinary! did you ever know any of that name?

Osb. Know any! God! yes; I did know *one* a long while since, in Europe. Was this Campdon ever there? [*Eagerly.*

Syd. Not within my recollection; and, since my father's death, I have never been from him. He has been the only parent I ever knew, and he has been a kind one.

Osb. Has he? [*With warmth.*

Syd. Oh, yes! he has, indeed, refused me his daughter. But by what right did I dare ask her? Already has the beggar Russel received too many favours from him.

Osb. Did he not drive you from his house?

Syd. Oh, no! I myself fled it; I wished not to be ungrateful. I wished to forget Louisa; but could not.

Osb. Noble boy! But your father; you said he died?

Syd. Alas! yes.

Osb. And left but you? No family? no—

Syd. Spare me; I had a sister.

Osb. Had! Is she dead?

Syd. To me; to the world; to virtue!

Osb. Unhappy girl! she had no father to guide her. But you live, Sydney; you live to virtue, to—

[*With great warmth.*

Syd. Sir?

Osb. (*Apart.*) Let me not be precipitate. Should my hopes mislead me! Russel! [*Musing.*

Syd. Sir, did you speak?

Osb. If it be so, the change of name is strange; is unaccountable.

Syd. Perhaps of Mrs. Freegrace I may receive some information. Will you accompany me thither, Mr. Osbert?

Osb. (*Still musing.*) Russel! it is impossible!

Syd. Then adieu, till we meet at our lodgings.

Osb. Stop! hold! no; by and by. (*Takes Sydney's hand.*) Sydney, return quickly.

Syd. The recital of his story has strangely disordered him.

Osb. I'll hasten to inquire concerning this Campdon; should it be—(*Going, returns.*) Return quickly, Sydney. Be sure!—

Syd. I cannot fail. [*Exit.*

Osb. If he has been in Hamburgh!—

[*Exit, disorderedly.*

Scene—*At Mrs. Clermont's*

Mrs. Clermont, *Widow* Freegrace

Wid. Fr. Pray, proceed.

Mrs. C. We are interrupted.

Enter Miss Starchington

Miss S. Positively, Mrs. Clermont, you have a most superb house here. I've made free to ramble all over it, from top to bottom.

Wid. Fr. I think you have made free, indeed, sister.

Miss S. Oh Lord! I know Mrs. Clermont is perfectly willing I should.

Mrs. C. I hope Miss Starchington will seek her own convenience and satisfaction here.

Miss S. Seek as I will, though, I can't be satisfied. These stupid servants know as little of their mistress as I do. (*Apart.*) That's an elegant harp in the next room. Do you play sometimes, madam?

Mrs. C. Sometimes.

Miss S. Ah! not often. I thought so; for 'tis shockingly out of tune.

Mrs. C. You are an amateur, then?

Miss S. Why, some partial friends have said, madam—

Wid. Fr. Sing, sister, and convince Mrs. Clermont of your musical talent.

Miss S. An unfortunate cold I caught last night; really I am an absolute raven this morning.

Wid. Fr. You won't? Why then I will; and though my voice may be as *unmusical* as the raven's, the similitude shall hold no farther, for it will bode no evil, but rather, if it can, chase away sorrow.

Song

Blithe Rosa beheld, as she sat in her cot,
An intruder the door open wide;

Her Edwy was absent: he knew it, he came,
'Twas Sorrow that stood by her side.
Yet she sang cheerily, get away, Sorrow!
Edwy will come ere the lark hails the morrow:
Where Edwy is, you can never be, Sorrow;
Get away, get away, Sorrow!

Just then Edwy enter'd, conducted by Love,
And he brought laughing Joy as his guest;
Gloomy Sorrow withdrew, all abash'd, from the place,
While the cottagers' song his flight prest.
While they sung cheerily, get away, Sorrow!
Hie to the guilty! and bid your good morrow;
But fly from the presence of Love and Joy, Sorrow!
Get away, get away, Sorrow!

And though oft returning for entrance he pleads,
Yet chas'd soon is Sorrow away,
When he taps at the casement, or lifts up the latch,
And his ears catch the cottagers' lay,
While they sing cheerily, get away, Sorrow!
Come not to day, demon! come not to morrow,
Virtue and Innocence know thee not, Sorrow;
Get away, get away, Sorrow!

Miss S. Ah! very tolerable; but why, sister, don't you learn the harp? There's such a field for a display of the graces. I'm told, madam, that, when seated at the harp, I look like—

Wid. Fr. Like the figure of David playing to Saul, in the wooden cut of a Dutch bible.

Miss S. *I* like a wooden cut. This is envy; believe it, madam, sheer envy; before she was bor—I mean before she was *married*, I had made an admirable proficiency in most of the elegant arts.

Mrs. C. Indeed?

Miss S. Yes, madam; not less in music than in shell-work; and equally great in poetry, dancing, botany, and French; and for painting, I always had the title of the western Angelica.

Wid. Fr. You'll pardon my not remembering those times, for, sister, as you say, I was not bor—

Miss S. Apropos to painting; you have some charming pictures, madam.

Mrs. C. I am glad you like them.

Miss S. One in particular I admire. 'Tis the head of a gentleman; very handsome, and, I dare say, done by Angelo, or Lavater, or some other great master. It hangs, madam, in a little room, all by itself, just as you—

Mrs. C. You have not been in that room?

Miss S. Madam, I hope—oh, is it so? (*Apart.*) I beg pardon if there's any thing particular, ma'am, but, upon my honour, I saw nothing but a picture.

Mrs. C. Nay, 'tis of no consequence.

Miss S. I won't leave it so, though—(*Aside.*) Without doubt, 'tis the most beautiful face I ever beheld.

Mrs. C. (*With suppressed emotion.*) Do you think so?

Miss S. Oh, yes, perfectly enchanting! such eyes! And I dare say you value it very highly, madam?

Mrs. C. I do.

Miss S. Your father, perhaps—

Mrs. C. No.

Miss S. Or husband, or some dear friend that's dead?

Mrs. C. Oh, no more! no more! [*Walks up in tears*

Miss S. So: I've found it out at last.

Wid. Fr. What have you found out?

Miss S. That she's a kept madam, and that that picture's the face of some other woman's husband.

Wid. Fr. Wonderful ingenuity! and what reason have you for this?

Miss S. Reason enough. Do you think she would weep thus for her own husband, or have his picture hung so snug out of the way?

Wid. Fr. I'm ashamed of you.

Enter Servant

Ser. Mr. Russel inquires for Mrs. Freegrace.

Wid. Fr. 'Tis Sydney. Have I your leave, madam?

Mrs. C. Command here, my dear Mrs. Freegrace.

Wid. Fr. Desire Mr. Russel to walk up. [*Exit servant.*

Mrs. C. I will retire.

Miss S. And so will I, when that beggar makes one.

Wid. Fr. Nay, stay, madam; this lover of Louisa's is very amiable.

Mrs. C. I am, at present, unfit for company. [*Exit.*

Miss S. Ay, ay! guilt and remorse.

Enter Sydney

He bows to Miss Starchington, whom he meets. She returns it superciliously, and exit

Syd. The poor orphan, I see, is not forgotten. Not finding you at your own house, madam, I have ventured—Do I intrude?

Wid. Fr. Intrude! my dear Sydney, a thousand times welcome.

Syd. The worthless thanks of one who has nothing else to offer are yours, madam.

Wid. Fr. But how you look! or rather, how you do not look! Where are your eyes? Hold up your head. Is that the air a naval hero should assume?

Syd. At least, 'tis the air a miserable dependent should wear.

Wid. Fr. Nonsense. Be a man.

Syd. I am a wretched one; racked, tortured beyond endurance. To night, madam, sees my hopes blasted for ever. And yet, can it be so? You know her; will you believe it? Can Louisa? Your pardon, madam; I rave; forgive me.

Wid. Fr. I tell you, be a man; hope, and listen to me.

Syd. As to an oracle—for you alone bid me hope, whilst all the world beside—

Wid. Fr. Hang the world! hear me. Louisa loves you.

Syd. And shall I lose her?

Wid. Fr. No. She is to be married to night—be quiet—but whether to yourself, or to Fluttermore, *you* must determine.

Syd. But how, my dear madam? By what means?

Wid. Fr. By eloping.

Syd. Eloping! would that be honourable?

Wid. Fr. Honourable! I hope, for the honour of a seaman, you are better acquainted with naval tactics than with those of love. Your gratitude, then, to the father, who has about half fulfilled his duty towards you, would bid you let the daughter, whose happiness depends on you, sigh out a miserable life in arms of a fopling whom she hates?

Syd. Oh, no—no. By Heaven! Fluttermore shall not so triumph!

Wid. Fr. Hasten then to Louisa; use all your rhetoric, and complete what I have begun, by persuading her to run away with you.

Syd. You have breathed new life into me, my best of friends.

Wid. Fr. Tolerably disinterested, for a widow: our sisterhood are not very famous for taking pains to throw handsome young fellows from them. But, away; the affair cries haste! don't speak, but begone. (*Exit Sydney.*) And if I can make two worthy souls happy, let the world rail on.

Enter Mrs. Clermont

Mrs. C. (*Entering.*) Oh God! that countenance!

Wid. Fr. You seem agitated, madam.

Mrs. C. The youth whom I met—

Wid. Fr. Sydney—what of him?

Mrs. C. Nay, perhaps 'twas only fancy. I am ever the sport of an imagination which constantly gives the form it loves even to shadows. Yet the resemblance—it seemed he himself!

Wid. Fr. Who?

Mrs. C. My husband; his very self. Tell me: that youth is an orphan?

Wid. Fr. Yes.

Mrs. C. He had—but why do I indulge these ideas—he had a sister?

Wid. Fr. He had. Of the same age.

Mrs. C. Ha! a vague, uncertain ray of hope dawns on me. I will welcome it; for the gloom of despair has held long enough. The likeness! the similiarity!—

Wid. Fr. My dear Mrs. Clermont, do not let a slight coincidence of circumstances lead your hopes too far. This young man's name is Russel.

Mrs. C. True; 'tis improbable. I will restrain my eager wishes.

Wid. Fr. And to night we can learn some particulars from Mr. Campdon. But my sister interrupted you in your interesting recital.

Mrs. C. But little remained. Freed from my prison, by the effects of the war, and accompanied by the faithful creature to whose ingenuity I was indebted for the safety of my jewels, I left the country where I no longer had a family, and arrived on these hospitable shores. To avoid impertinent attention, I resumed my family name; and, notwithstanding the most unremitting inquiries, for many long years have lived without hope—till to day—But no; I will not again trust Fortune. I will be indifferent.

Wid. Fr. Ah, my dear madam—

Mrs. C. I will. My soul shall be at rest.

[*Very much agitated. Exeunt.*

Scene—*Osbert's lodgings*

Osbert, *sitting*

'Tis certain, then. Heaven has again smiled on me, and the brave Sydney is my son! But his mother! His sister! Ungrateful murmurer! I am a father; be that assured bliss mine. Oh! I already feel a son's embrace; already I see the drops of filial tenderness glisten lovelily; and hear the ever harmonious voice of nature speak in its sweetest tone, as a child greets for the first time his parent. But, alas! what parent do I bring him? Is it not one who will but shame him, who will but mar his every prospect? Campdon was once my friend; but age has crept through his veins; and his commerce with a cold world has deadened each finer feeling of the soul. He will not know me as his friend. My son cannot be his son. What then remains? 'Till this marriage is concluded, you shall be happily ignorant, Sydney, that you have a wretched father in existence, whose poverty would only remove farther from you the object of your wishes. He comes!

Enter Sydney

Sydney, (*Taking his hand*) you look smilingly.

Syd. I have cause. Hope has revisited me. Will you ride a few miles?

Osb. Willingly.

Syd. Come. And now, good genius of lovers, grant me but an interview!

Osb. An interview? You are determined then to pursue this shadow that still flies you?

Syd. As constantly as I do my own. The meridian sun of fortune may shine, and I shall overtake the shadow.

Osb. But, Sydney—

Syd. Nay, no philosophy. I die with impatience.

Osb. Say, at least, whence do these hopes arise?

Syd. You shall know all when we're mounted. Come.

[*Exeunt.*

Act IV.

Scene—*A landscape, some distance from General Campdon's country house*

Enter Clara, *with a child*

Come on, my boy, a little farther. Yes; I will see Louisa; her generous soul will pity and forgive me. You have made your mother's arms ache, my innocent cherub, but your unkind father has wrung her heart! Tremble not, guilty Edward; I will not rob you of your bride. The abandoned Clara comes from the solitude whither shame and infamy had driven her, but to bid you protect your son; to forgive you, and die. The day declines fast; till to-morrow, I will ask a shelter of General Campdon: his villa cannot be far distant, for, alas! its precincts I know but too well. Here, in my days of innocence, I have wandered with him who—but 'tis past! Let us proceed my love; I will gain strength soon again, to carry my precious burthen.

[*Exit, with child.*

Scene—*General Campdon's grounds. A view of the villa*

Camp. (*Within*) Ah, mighty pretty, indeed.

Gal. O *oui,* yes; beautiful, yes—

Enter General, *followed by Mr.* Campdon.

Gen. Then here, you observe, in this spot—why don't you come on, Mr. Galliard?

Galliard *enters, with reluctance, looking behind*

Gal. *Permettez moi,* I vill vait for de lady.

Gen. Pshaw! the lady's coming. Then here, do you see, this spot I mean to plant full of trees.

Gal. Ah, yes, full— [*Looking the other way.*

Gen. Yes, but not there. Then I shall cut all *those* down; *those* you see, M. Galliard. [*Turning him round.*

Gal. *Ah, bon;* yes, cut all down; ver good.

Camp. But why, brother, cut all of them down, and plant this place full?

Gen. Why? Why because there are too many there, and none here at all, to be sure.

Camp. I'm satisfied.

Gen. And there, monsieur, runs my canal.

Gal. I see, yes— [*His back still toward him.*

Gen. Do ye? Then you must have a looking-glass before you. This way, monsieur, there runs—

Gal. Oh, de lady.

Gen. The devil she does; why, M. Galliard, you don't pay any attention.

Camp. Perhaps the gentleman is fatigued—as I am. (*Apart.*) Suppose, brother, we return?

Gen. Return? Why you hav'n't seen half my improvements. You are not fatigued, M. Galliard?

Gal. Oh no—*pas fatigué*, I am ravished.

Gen. Well, now we'll walk on to the canal.

Gal. As I hope to be save, I vish you vas walk *into* it!

[*Apart.*

Gen. Come on, monsieur; don't lag; come—

Gal. *Très volontiers*—(*Shrugs discontentedly, looking behind.*) [*Exeunt.*

Enter Fluttermore *and* Louisa; Rangely *following*

Flut. Isn't it a most incomparably ridiculous story, my dear? O, poor Jack! ha, ha! can't you fancy you see him, Louisa; eyes and mouth wide staring, arms dangling, and his whole form gracefully stiff, as might be a copy of the Apollo Belvidere, by an American stone-cutter! ha, ha! and in imminent danger of dying a martyr to love, under the wheels of her ladyship's carriage?

Ran. Oh, curse it, Ned, this is not friendly; I looked for commiseration, not derision. How kind it is in you, ma'am, not, to laugh! nay, don't smile. That's at least a demi-mock.

Lou. You mistake its meaning; I smiled to think how surprized my friend Freegrace will be to night at a sight of her dumb deliverer, as she calls you.

Ran. How? Your friend? To night? My dear ma'am, do you know her? Shall I see her? Has she told you? Does she remember me? Answer, in pity, madam.

Flut. In thunder, you mean, if she wishes to be heard: and is it possible that all this fuss was about little Freegrace?

Ran. Do you know her too, Ned? Happy fellow! Isn't she a divinity?

Fut. Only half a one. Her moiety was mere mortal, and died one day; she's a widow.

Ran. She's an angel.

Flut. She's a tartar.

Lou. You wrong her; Mrs. Freegrace has wit and spirit, but her mind is as free from asperity as her person is from fault. She's a charming woman, whom I am proud to call my friend.

Ran. She is, she must be perfection; my dear madam, how happy you've made me; what, to-night! oh "gallop apace, ye fiery-footed steeds!"

Flut. La, la, la! [*Singing.*

Ran. But egad—I'm not quite sure; pray, madam, do you think such a scape-grace as myself—that is, do you happen to recollect among her lovers (for she must have millions) such a thing as a favoured, a particular, a—

Lou. I am certain—none.

Ran. She's mine; I feel it; I am married.

Flut. Feel it! what are the symptoms? A *mal de tête?* Do your brows branch by anticipation?

Lou. I'll join my uncle— [*Going.*

Ran. Nay, Fluttermore, your wit's as offensive as 'tis trite. Faith, madam, my friend Ned don't deserve such loveliness. A man with his gross ideas of the sex is not worthy of so fair a proof of their being erroneous.

Flut. Gallantly conceived, that; and exprest *passablement bien.* But, my dear, you must not mind these trifles. You must have different ideas when we go to Europe.

Lou. When we go to Europe I may, sir. Familiar fop!

[*Turns away.*

Ran. Hey, Ned?

Flut. Miff: those horns have sounded an alarm to the girl's modesty. Your widow's different, Jack; knows a thing; if you get her, she'll shine in Europe.

Ran. No, I have done rambling; if I get her, she shall shine only in this hemisphere.

Flut. What, you'll *settle,* as the phrase is—*dans ce pays-ci?*

Ran. Yes.

Flut. Turn sober citizen?

Ran. Ay.

Flut. And, *possibly,* go into business to improve your fortune?

Ran. Possibly.

Flut. *O Dieu!* what d'ye think, Louisa, of Jacky's sage plan?

Lou. That, with Mrs. Freegrace, it would ensure him rational happiness.

Flut. Ration—Oh infinite. *Ecoutez!* I'll tell you. Once a week or so, you'll emerge from the elegant cares of your counting-room, to take the benefit of the dust with spousy, to your rural cot on the high road; and once a year catch an ague, for the benefit of your health, at some one of your brilliant watering places. Amiably domestic, you'll play cards for kisses with lovey; or make one of a tea-drinking circle in the American taste; staring at each other like a room full of wax-figures; and gloomy as a Presbyterian synod.

Ran. Admirable!

Flut. You don't dance, therefore madam's annual cotillion is nothing to you; but you'll visit your unparalleled theatre, perhaps once a winter, to see some delectable American muse, in the shape of a comedy; and end the year merrily at Christmas, by settling your books, and collecting your debts.

Ran. You've drawn a pretty picture.

Lou. I see my uncle beckons. Shall we join him?

Flut. True, egad, I forgot. We came to see his improvements, if I recollect. Give me leave, my dear—

[*Hands her out; Rangely is following.*

Enter Yank

Yank. Mr. Rangely! Mr. Rangely! [*Pulling him.*

Ran. (*Turning.*) Yank! why how came you here?

Yank. A horseback.

Ran. But how did you find—

Yank. Oh, I asked every body for General Campdon's willow! But I've news, sir; she's found: Cognita's found!

Ran. I know it.

Yank. Now do ye? why, lord, who could tell ye?

Ran. I shall see her to night, you rogue! To night I shall see my lovely widow.

Yank. Now is she a widow? Then it wer she that he meant, sure enough.

Ran. Who meant?

Yank. Why, the gentleman that I wanted to follow here, ony his horse went faster nor mine. Him that she smiled so on when they were walking.

Ran. Smile! did she smile?

Yank. Lord, yes—tarnal sweet. But I must tell you: ater you left me, all in a puzzle as 'twer, out comes he, and, says he, I'm sorry to leave my sweet widow, but, says he, I must canter to Campdon's willow. So, says I, that's the very place my master's at, says I, and I'll follow you; so I run—no, first she put her head out of a window, and then I run to tell you what she said.

Ran. And what did she say?

Yank. Why she know'd me; and, says she, how d'ye do Yank; only think.

Ran. Was that all, idiot?

Yank. Thank ye.

Ran. Smile! did she smile! His sweet widow, did he call her? Furies! But who—

Yank. Never budge, if this an't him coming yan—

Ran. O'Connor. These devilish Irish!

Enter O'Connor

O'Con. Devil take me, Mr. Rangely, if I'm not glad to see ye, for faith I can see no soul beside. It was very ungenteel of them to leave me staring at an ugly picture over the chimney, without taking me with them at all. By the powers, next time I come out of town to be treated so scurvily, I'll make it a point to stay with my sweet little widow, who'll treat me much better.

Yank. There, sir.

Ran. Tortures! you're mistaken, sir, she'll treat you much worse.

O'Con. What?

Ran. She *shall* treat you worse, sir.

O'Con. Now, what the devil are you driving at?

Ran. Mine is the better right to her. I'll have her.

O'Con. Is it my widow you're speaking about?

Ran. Death, sir, she's my widow; she never smiled on you; she frowned. I'll swear she frowned.

O'Con. By the powers, he's mad.

Ran. And you must relinquish your pretensions.

O'Con. Relinquish! hark ye, young gentleman—if I can glean a grain of meaning from this harvest of nothing—you have a little bit of a liking for the lady in question.

Ran. Sir, I adore her, and—

O'Con. Stay a bit; be asy; now I happen to adore her too; so we jostle a little: well, we can't both together be the happy man. Suppose then we leave it, in a friendly way, to a couple of arbitrators.

Ran. Arbitrators?

O'Con. Yes—to be sure, they are leaden headed little gentlemen, but they come to a mighty swift decision—pop—at once.

Ran. I understand you; pistols?

O'Con. You've hit it.

Yank. O Lord! you'd better leave it to a justice of the peace.

Ran. Silence! Name the time and place, sir.

O'Con. Faith, now's the best *time;* but for place, let me see—we mustn't let the peaceable gentleman your servant mentioned hear the arguments of our referees.

Ran. 'Tis but stepping into the next state. Yank, you'll attend us.

Yank. What! into the next state? I an't afear'd to die, sir, only going so lightly into another state, without knowing whether its a blessed state or no—

Ran. Simpleton, I only want ye to cross the Delaware with me.

O'Con. Ay, only to step over the river. It's mighty easy, sure.

Yank. It must take a tarnal long stride to do it.

Ran. Come, sir, let it be this instant; the night will overtake us else. We can now go unobserved by the company.

O'Con. Faith, with all my heart.

[*Exeunt Rangely and O'Connor.*

Yank. O Lord, what is this world coming to! But I'll fix ye, if there's such a thing as a justice or constable in this here town. [*Exit.*

Enter Louisa

I have at last escaped from that impertinent fop, and have a few moments for reflection. Shall I then chuse misery, and obey my father? Filial duty, at whose voice every selfish consideration should be hushed, bids me do it. But will justice sanction such a decision? Have I the right to doom Sydney to misery with myself? Impossible! Reason—love—all forbid it.

Osbert *and* Sydney *appear behind*

Syd. 'Tis she. Mr. Osbert—

Osb. I understand you, my young friend. I will retire. But be prudent, and be brief too. I will wait near you.

[*Exit.*

Lou. I would Sydney were here. His honourable soul would conceive, and his noble candour would inform me how I should act.

Sydney come forward

Syd. Louisa!

Lou. Heavens!

Syd. Louisa!

Lou. (*Sees him.*) Ah, Sydney!

Syd. (*Running to embrace her.*) My Louisa!

Lou. (*Avoiding it.*) Oh, no! no!

Syd. Miss Campdon—am I unwelcome.

Lou. Most—most welcome.

Syd. Yet you avoid me—

Lou. Ah! should I not? Sydney, to night I become the wife of another.

Syd. The bargain then is concluded, and you have agreed to the mercenary arrangement?

Lou. Shall I, by refusing, make a father miserable?

Syd. By no means; consent, and make your father happy. Bless, also, this coxcomb lover; and for me—my miseries are nothing.

Lou. Unkind! And are mine less acute? Sydney, have I deserved this?

Syd. Forgive me—

Lou. I did not expect reproaches from you; nay, I hoped that the same generous pride which once drove you from me would approve my conduct now, and that yourself, with the hand of honour, would lead me into the path of duty.

Syd. And will. There wanted but this. Louisa, from infancy you have been fastened to my heart. You have grown to it; you are a part of it. Perhaps it will be somewhat difficult and painful to tear you thence—but it shall be done!

[*Wildly.*

Lou. Shall it?

Syd. Henceforth, when we meet, if ever we do again, we meet as strangers. You will not know *me.* I must not see *you.* Is't not so?

Lou. Sydney, how wildly you talk?

Syd. Louisa, you are right; you are a dutiful, a grateful daughter. Marry, Louisa, and pay the debt due your father! Shun me; you owe me nothing; forget me.

Lou. Forget you?

Syd. And now, farewell!

Lou. Sydney!

Syd. For ever!

Lou. Oh, never! never! Sydney, I am yours!

[*Rushing to him.*

Syd. I am a beggar.

Lou. I will share your poverty! I am yours.

Syd. Shall I take you from the bosom of Affluence, to place you in the cold, unfriendly arms of Penury? Oh! you would curse me for it.

Lou. Curse you?

Syd. No home, no friends to give you! think Louisa; despised, avoided.

Lou. Oh no; it is not so. Things may change; my father may relent.

Syd. If you but deceive yourself?

Lou. If I do, then be my friends, my home, my riches centered here; you shall be all to me.

Syd. My best love, the actions of a life will but poorly speak my gratitude.

Lou. Then to night—I will fly.

Syd. To night! are you not to be sacrificed to night?

Lou. My father shall defer it; I will feign, I will promise—

Syd. But why not this instant?

Lou. Impossible—even now, every moment, I dread—heavens! my father! to night—in the garden—

Enter General *and* Mr. Campdon

Camp. Hey day—who? Sydney! oh, the devil!

Gen. Ah! welcome home, my hero— [*Sydney bows.*

Syd. Mr. Campdon, I wished to pay my respects in town; but hearing you were here—

Camp. You come, post haste, to see *me!* Ah, very pretty that, and very true. Thank ye; I didn't expect ye quite so soon; you're welcome! Hark ye, Miss Campdon—

Gen. So, you banged the Tripoline. Come you must tell me about it. [*Walk up.*

Camp. Come hither, hussey; answer me without disguise: what did he say to you? What did you say to him? How long has he been here? What have ye agreed upon? How are ye to cheat your father? ha—

Lou. (*Assuming a girlish air.*) Lord, pa, you ask one so many questions.

Camp. I'll be answered, miss—

Lou. Which interrogatory first, sir?

Camp. How long has he been here?

Lou. But a few minutes.

Camp. One comfort, I came so unexpectedly, you hadn't time to form a plot; I suppose you'd scarce done hugging. Come to the house. Brother, will you go? Good bye, Sydney;

I shall be glad to see you at my house next week or so. At present, Sydney, as you have paid your respects, and have no other business, probably you couldn't do better than return to town.

Gen. Brother, you'll recollect Mr. Russel is my guest.

Camp. Oh, is he so? It follows then that he is to run away with my daughter. Very well! invite him to stay, and you bid me go; that's all.

Syd. I will not be the cause of any difference; permit me to take my leave.

Gen. You're a devilish clever fellow, Sydney; worth a thousand Fluttermores; and hark ye, if you can contrive to run away with her, I say nothing; but my doors here will not be locked, that's all.

Camp. Come along. Good bye, Sydney, you're a good lad, but my daughter is engaged. So good bye, till next week or so.

[*Exeunt Mr. Campdon, General, and Louisa.*

Syd. Next week! before that time, old man, you shall know me for your son. I'll instantly to town and arrange a plan.

Enter Osbert

Osb. A plan! For what?

Syd. Mr. Osbert, Hope did not flatter. To night sees the completion of my proudest wishes.

Osb. Has, then, the father consented?

Syd. No: but the daughter has.

Osb. To an elopement?

Syd. Yes.

Osb. And can you consent to it?

Syd. My Louisa demands it.

Osb. You should refuse it. Has every sense of honour left your breast?

Syd. Every false idea of it has. Every chilling maxim of cold preciseness, which serves but to paralize nature, has left it, and Love alone holds dominion! warm, glowing, benevolent Love! Love that blesses, while it is blessed.

Osb. How naturally allied is passion with sophistry!

Syd. And how natural to condemn in age what we practised in youth! You were once a lover, Mr. Osbert.

Osb. I would steer you from the rock upon which I split.

Syd. Adventuring for Louisa, sir, I am not to be appalled by danger.

Osb. And, to gratify your ungovernable passion, you would make a lovely young creature miserable?

Syd. Not so; to ensure her a moment of felicity, I would sacrifice my life.

Osb. Sacrifice your happiness, then, in this instance.

Syd. So should I her's; it is interwoven with mine.

Osb. She loves you?

Syd. Yes.

Osb. And for that reason you would reduce her to beggary?

Syd. We will be content, though not rich. I am young; I can labour.

Osb. Love in a cottage! what fallacious imagery does this blind limner, Love, depict. Still consider, Sydney. Campdon has been kind to you.

Syd. But he is unkind to his daughter.

Osb. And you would steal into his house? Where is your dignity of mind? You would become a robber?

Syd. Ay, by heaven! when force kept from me my own.

Osb. Is *she* yours?

Syd. Yes; with her heart she gave me herself.

Osb. She had not the power, she is her father's.

Syd. Till to night—to night she shall be mine.

[*Warmly.*

Osb. She shall not.

Syd. Sir!

Osb. That is; if you—consider rightly.

Syd. Let me consider as I please to night; and, to borrow an expression of Mr. Campdon, do with me what you please "next week." Mr. Osbert, I acknowledge the value of your friendship, and, but in this one instance, command me ever.

Osb. You make me physician with a singular diploma. To practise after my patient is dead. But I must convince you of your error yet.

Syd. You must first change right to wrong.

Osb. No; I'll only change your ideas of them. [*Exeunt.*

Scene—*An open wood—Twilight*

Enter Fluttermore

Confound these improvements of my guardian's! The fatigue of tramping over them absolutely laid me rustically asleep under a tree. Heigh ho! what the devil's the matter with me! Egad, if it wasn't so vulgar to be superstitious, I'm disposed to be infernally low spirited. Poor Clara—where are you wandering? Perhaps dead—

Cla. (*Passing through.*) Weary, weary to death.

Flut. Who said death? Pshaw, I'm not such an idiot. But the woods—and something here; a conscience, or—

Cla. (*As she goes out.*) Oh, Edward, what have you made me suffer! [*Exit.*

Flut. What—mercy—am I awake—Clara—just God, Clara!

Enter Monsieur Galliard

Who's that?

Gal. A ha, monsieur Fluttermore, I have *cherché* you. *Que le diable!* you ave de fright on your face!

Flut. Did you see nothing pass you?

Gal. No, only de little bird as it fly home to bed.

Flut. By heaven, 'twas Clara.

Gal. What, in de shape of de little bird; *ma foi,* I ave not such *bon fortune* to meet dat same *mademoiselle Claire.* *Mon ami,* you ave had de dream, *je crois.*

Flut. If I live, I saw her.

Gal. So did not myself.

Flut. I am bewildered.

Gal. Yes—ve are both bewilder in de wood. Two babes in the wood, *ma foi!* En bien! let us begone.

[*Exeunt.*

Act V

Scene—*At Mr. Campdon's*

Louisa *and* Clara

Cla. I was not deceived. I knew your gentle heart, when you were acquainted with the base arts that were used, would pity and forgive me.

Lou. From my soul I do. Your situation claims, and shall have, my tenderest commiseration and protection.

Cla. Generous Louisa!

Lou. But why persist in your refusal to name the author of your wrongs?

Cla. I have only delayed the discovery through a fear—

Lou. A fear of what?

Cla. You are concerned in the discovery, Louisa.

Lou. I concerned!

Camp. (*Within.*) But where's the bridegroom?

Lou. My father's voice!

Cla. Oh! I cannot meet him; suffer me to retire.

Lou. Go, my dear girl; I will see you immediately.

[*Exit Clara.*

Enter Campdon

Camp. Have you seen Fluttermore?

Lou. No, sir.

Camp. What can the stupid fellow have done with himself on the night of his wedding? Wasn't that Clara that parted from you? What did she run away for?

Lou. She was ashamed to meet you, sir.

Camp. And well she might—a little slippery jade! What did you bring her here for?

Lou. Should I have let her and her infant perish in the fields, sir?

Camp. Hum! No: but you'll be disgraced; my house will be disgraced; for she's a—

Lou. A victim to the fraud of a villain.

Camp. Ah! pretty terms these moderns have invented! But to-morrow I'll send her to her brother; they'll make a handsome pair. Who comes here? Pshaw! that old—

Enter Miss Starchington

Miss S. Mr. Campdon, your devoted servant. Louisa, my dear, there's Mrs. Clermont and my sister just entering.

Lou. I'll hasten to receive them. [*Exit.*

Camp. O Lord! O Lord! two widows in my house at a time!

Miss S. You are not fond of widows, then, Mr. Campdon?

Camp. Fond! I hate them as bad—as bad as I do old maids. [*Aside.*

Miss S. I applaud your taste, for they're generally but malapert things; but a widower—I think I could love a widower.

Camp. Do ye?

Miss S. Yes. That is, a staid, sober gentleman, with just years enough on his back to give him solidity: about your age, Mr. Campdon.

Camp. My age!

Miss S. By the way, now your daughter is to be married, you'll doubtless feel very lonesome without a female companion to soothe ye, to nurse ye, to prattle—

Camp. Prattle! O Lord—Ah! isn't that Fluttermore just come in? Excuse me, Miss Starchington. [*Exit.*

Miss S. Stupid old brute! The men are absolutely all

blocks. No sensibility; no feeling. Ah! the charming Frenchman!

Enter Galliard

Gal. (*Aside.*) Oh, *le diable!* de old maiden!—Hem! Ah, madame, I am happy to—you are alone? I thought de ladies—

Miss S. Ah, Mr. Galliard! tender thoughts cannot be well indulged in a crowd. The heart that loves always prefers solitude, unless the beloved object be present.

Gal. Ah, you fair *solitaire,* you vish to sigh to yourself. *Je suis faché*—I am very sorry for interrupt your tender tought— [*Going.*

Miss S. Why, you're not going, Mr. Galliard? I didn't say I wished for solitude now; for when the beloved object is present, Mr. Galliard—Oh, lud, my tongue! what have I uttered?

Gal. Uttered! 'pon my honare—permit me, madame— [*Presents snuff.*

Miss S. Heavens! can a Frenchman be so dull? Your friend Fluttermore is going to be very happy, Mr. Galliard?

Gal. O *oui,* yes—ver happy. I vish—

Miss S. Do you—do you wish to taste the joys of connubial love?

Gal. Connubi—a—

Miss S. Suppose a foolish young creature was "pining in thought" for you; one who "never told her love, but let concealment, like a worm i' the bud, feed on her damask cheek:" would you pity her? Would you marry—

Gal. O yes; if it was—

Miss S. Ah!—Well!—

Gal. Suppose it was the lit quake gal—

Miss S. Pshaw!

Gal. Vil ve join de company?

Miss S. Quaker, indeed! the tasteless wretch! [*Exeunt.*

Scene—*Another apartment*

Louisa *and* Clara

Cla. Edward now in the house?

Lou. He passed me this moment; but so agitated that he did not observe me. He has certainly seen you, or learned something—but see, he comes this way.

Cla. This way! Oh, heaven!

Lou. Nay, nay; compose yourself. Meet him with firmness, and win him back to honour.

Cla. Oh, impossible! can I meet *him* with firmness who has reduced me to the lowest state of wretchedness? or can *he* be brought to feel a sentiment of honour, who could so cruelly abandon his innocent child? Oh, let me fly—

Lou. Not for the world! You mentioned your child. Will you not make one effort to give that infant a father? Think, too, of the consequences when your brother hears—He comes; collect your spirits, my dear Clara.

Cla. But you will not leave me? [*They retire up.*

Enter Fluttermore

Flut. 'Tis so, then. The innocent, the lovely Clara is wandering, an unprotected outcast. And I—what a rascal am I! But this instant I will begin my search. If she can be found —(*Louisa meets him.*) Miss Campdon, I—I have been rather tardy in paying my respects; but—

Lou. That is easily pardoned, for I have no claim to them; but how will you account for your three years' guilty negligence of one to whom all your respect, your most tender attentions were due?

Flut. What do you mean? Have you seen—Whom do you allude to?

Lou. Look at that lady.

[*Pointing to Clara, who is slowly retiring.*

Flut. Heaven and earth! it is Clara!

Lou. Yes; the injured Clara, whose heart you have almost broken. If you are a man, hasten and make the only reparation now in your power.

Flut. (*As he goes out.*) How shall I approach? For pity's sake, Miss Campdon—what can I say? Louisa, won't you intercede?

Lou. Nay, follow—

Flut. How like a wretch I feel! [*Exit.*

Lou. O powerful guilt! which can even transform the pert fop into the awkward clown.—Ah! he is at her feet! He seizes her hand! So, all will be well, I hope; and now for my own affair. I must at least see Sydney. [*Exit.*

Scene—*The garden of Mr. Campdon.—An arbour on each side. —Moonlight*

Enter Osbert *and* Sydney

Osb. You are then determined—

Syd. So determined that all your eloquence is useless. We are now in the garden, and in a few moments—

Osb. Cannot I dissuade you?

Syd. Never; therefore use no more words—

Osb. Yes; one word more: I *command* you to desist.

Syd. *Command* me! This is a stretch of authority somewhat beyond the limits our friendship allows. Sir, by what right do you *command* me?

Osb. By a privilege granted me by Nature; by a right which Heaven recognizes as sacred, which it would be impious to oppose.

Syd. Amazement! what do you mean?

Osb. Are these emotions then equivocal? Does Nature hold a language unintelligible? Do a parent's arms expand in vain to infold his child?

Syd. Do I hear? parent!

Osb. Sydney Osbert!

Syd. Ah!

Osb. My son!

Syd. Just God! Father! [*Rushes into his father's arms.*

Osb. My boy!

Syd. Have I then a parent? Oh, my father, what have been your sufferings! wandering neglected through an unfeeling world! and your son ignorant of your being, incapable of sharing, of alleviating your afflictions! Let then my future life be devoted to you, my father; and every action be made sacred by your service! Be this embrace the pledge.

Osb. I receive the pledge—I test your faithfulness. Sydney, renounce this clandestine union!

Syd. My father!

Osb. Can you repay the kindness of a patron with perfidy? Can you bring the shame of ingratitude on yourself, on your father? Do not—do not call down a parent's malediction on the woman whom you love, who loves you—as I have done! Do not inflict beggary and shame on your hapless children, as I have done!

Syd. Ah!

Osb. Your mother is dead, Sydney; and your sister—I have but you alone. Will *you* prove unworthy? Shall I curse the day that restored to me my son?

Syd. (*After a struggle.*) Father, I am yours; what would you have me do?

Osb. Quit this garden with me.

Syd. And not see Louisa?

Osb. See her; tell her you have found a parent; and return to receive that parent's blessing. To morrow we will see Mr. Campdon; we will thank him for his favours, and retire to virtuous poverty together.

Syd. 'Tis done. I offered you my life; I will surrender what is dearer!

Osb. You will find me without.

Syd. (*Hesitating.*) But, my father! (*Osbert waves his hand.*) Oh Louisa! [*Exeunt, severally.*

Rangely *appears on the garden wall*

Ah, so—now—(*Jumps down*) here I am safe! They followed dev'lish close, though. That infernal Yank! to give information of our duel, and send me scampering thus over walls, at the hazard of my neck! Then the night to come on so suddenly, and prevent our crossing the river! What an unlucky dog am I! Just as I was about to be blest with a sight of my lovely widow—Hey! by the girdle of Venus! a petticoat! Couch! [*Retires.*

Enter Widow Freegrace

Wid. Fr. No where to be found! possibly she has already met Sydney, and left the garden. That stupid game of whist! I would have given the world to have thrown up my cards, and witnessed the interview.

Ran. Oh Apollo! there is but one mouth in the universe can emit these dulcet sounds!

Wid. Fr. I take a great deal of trouble about these lovers. I wish some good-natured person would return the compliment, and send me that dumb deliverer of mine!

Ran. Meaning me. "Shall I hear more?"

Wid. Fr. Hang the fellow! his neglect is unaccountable: when he might have a young and rich widow for the asking!

Ran. (*Coming forward.*) "I take thee at thy word! call me but love, and I'll no longer be a batchelor!"

Wid. Fr. Heavens! who are you, sir?

Ran. Honest Jack Rangely, madam; whom your charms once struck dumb; but who has borrowed, this moment, from your entrancing words, just power of speech sufficient to say and swear, he loves, he adores you.

Wid. Fr. Mr. Rangely! why, good heavens, how did you come here?

Ran. " With love's light wings did I o'erperch yon walls."

Wid. Fr. And why not come soberly into the house by the door? Miss Campdon bade me expect you to night.

Ran. Campdon! and is this garden then—

Wid. Fr. So! you don't know where you are! you borrow the wings of Love, then, to fly over a strange wall! Oh you men! you men!

Ran. Gad, I'm caught; but faith, madam, after all, I told half a truth. Love and Fear each lent me a wing. Fear sent me here to avoid the effects of a duel; but Love made me fight that duel!

Wid. Fr. Is it possible? A duel! with whom? For what?

Ran. True, indeed! with my rival O'Connor; for you.

Wid. Fr. You terrify me.

Ran. Don't be alarmed, madam; I'm too bad a shot to have done mischief, though I chose to run away from the tedious formalities of the law, the rather as I expected the happiness of seeing you to night. And bless the little god who bid me jump over here, for I've heard—you can't deny it—like Romeo, I listened; like Juliet, you confessed. You must have me. You will; say you will.

Wid. Fr. Heaven help the man, how he runs on! Why, I expected a modest, speechless kind of a body; but I can't get a word in! Lord! d'ye think I'll marry a man who talks more than myself?

Ran. I'm dumb, madam; dumb, as when you first knew me. I'll be eternally dumb, if you'll promise always to be talking, for your voice—(*She smiles*) a hem!

Wid. Fr. What a *babillard!*

Ran. Cure me, madam. Marry me.

Wid. Fr. They say you're a sad rake!

Ran. Love has half reformed me; let Hymen complete the good work. Marry me.

Wid. Fr. The hazard would be too great: for, if I took you, what assurance could I have of keeping such a rover?

Ran. Nay, dear madam, don't make me out quite so great a fool as Lucifer: to run from Heaven!

Wid. Fr. Rodomontade!

Ran. Plain matter of fact. For what but heaven would be my snug comfortable parlour, where an *angel* would smile by my side, while a parcel of rosy little *cherubs* laughed at my feet?

Wid. Fr. Nonsense!

Ran. Consent! (*Seizing her hand*) consent!

Miss S. (*Within.*) "Moon, ah moon!"

Ran. "Moon, ah moon!" Is that a lunatic, madam?

Wid. Fr. An old maid, only. I must disappear, or she'll have eternal food for railing. Why, you wretch! you are not going to follow me?

Ran. Good God! my dear madam, would you leave me all alone, with an old maid, who apostrophizes the moon?

[*Rangely follows the widow into an arbour.*

Enter Miss Starchington *and* Galliard

Miss S. Let me see. The next lines—

Gal. By de lor! I tink de ole vitch as conjure me. I cannot get loose. [*Apart.*

Miss S. Oh! I recollect. Thus it concludes, with a tolerable antithesis:

Be wrapt, ah moon! all in a black cloud!
For, Ah! my love's wrapt in a white shroud!

What do you think of my ode to the moon, Mr. Galliard.

Gal. Oh! de poem, de subject, de auteur, are all alike: shaste an beautiful.

Miss S. Ah! you're so flattering! Does it, indeed, move you?

Gal. Vis all my soul I wish it could—fifty hunder mile from you. (*Aside*) A hem! so pathetique!

Miss S. Yet 'tis only from the fancy, for it was written before I knew the *belle passion.* What would be an effusion of the same muse now, Mr. Galliard, where the low breathings of passionate complaint should be addressed to a too alluring foreigner, who led astray my virgin heart? Oh heaven! company moves this way! Step into this arbour, till they pass.

Gal. Step in! For vy? By de lor, I love de compagné.

Miss S. Oh, my reputation, Mr. Galliard! my virgin fame! To be found thus with a man!

Gal. I vill run away!

Miss S. That would be worse: you'd be seen. Come in. 'Tis so dark, no one can discover us.

Gal. Dark! have you not afraid?

Miss S. Not with you. Quick, quick!

[*Exeunt into arbour.*

Enter Sydney *and* Louisa

Syd. By Heaven! he shall meet a punishment, prompt and signal, as the wretch who betrays confiding innocence deserves!

Lou. For my sake, Sydney, be less rash; at least, do not treat Clara with harshness. In bitterness of soul she implored me to intercede for her.

Syd. Louisa, your commands would soften a far more rugged disposition than mine. Clara shall still be my sister; but for Fluttermore—

Camp. (*Within.*) I tell you, she's off.

Syd. Your father!

Lou. We will not avoid him. This event must certainly prevent the marriage; and, perhaps—

Enter General Campdon, *Mr.* Campdon, Fluttermore, *and* Clara

Camp. There! what did I say?

Syd. (*Going up to Fluttermore.*) Sir, you are a villain!

Flut. Rather a harsh word that, brother, to bestow on the husband of your sister!

Syd. Husband?

Gen. Yes, my fine fellow; the reverend gentleman within has done that friendly office for them.

Flut. But still I do not consider that I have made the *amende honorable*, until the most unremitting tenderness shall have proved, that the unfeeling coxcomb has become an affectionate husband.

Syd. (*Taking a hand of each.*) I am happy.

Gen. You shall be happier; for now, you know, brother, you'll give him Louisa.

Camp. Are your sure of that? (*To Sydney.*) Pray, sir, how can you dare look me in the face, after an attempt to run away with my daughter, which only my coming prevented?

Syd. You are mistaken; your coming did not prevent it.

Camp. No! what did then?

Syd. I'll show you. [*Exit.*

Camp. What does he mean?

Lou. He has found a father.

Clar. A father! oh heaven!

Lou. A truly honourable one, who forbade Sydney to—

Camp. To run away with you; contrary to your wishes, I dare say, hussey. It was well done, however; and since Fluttermore is married, and Sydney a pretty clever lad, and you love him, why—

Lou. My dear, dear sir.

Camp. But I am impatient to see this unknown friend.

Clara. And I to see a father.

[*Rangely and widow come from the arbour.*

Ran. Nothing to fear, my love.

Flut. Hillo! "These turtles two came from the bower." [*Singing.*

Ran. Joy, ma'am! joy, miss! joy, Ned! and give me joy too, for she's mine.

Gen. Is this so, widow?

Wid. Fr. Yes: the teazing creature has "wrung from me my slow leave."

Ran. Talking of turtles, there are a pair in yonder arbour—full-fledg'd too, egad!

Miss S. (*In the arbour.*) But, Mr. Galliard—

[*Galliard enters, followed by Miss Starchington.*

Gen. The male turtle flies—

Wid. Fr. And the female follows.

Camp. Natural enough.

Miss S. What amends can you make, you wounder of my virgin fame?

Gal. *Mesdames et messieurs*, ladies an gentlesmen, I assure you I ave not wound her virgin fame. I ave not touch any ting about her.

Camp. You must marry her, Galliard.

Gal. You vill excuse me; I vill more soon marry my *grand mere.* Ma foi! I vill only marry de lit quake.

Wid. You forget, sister, that I overheard your dialogue. O fie! are these your notions of propriety?

O'Con. (*Speaks within.*) Upon my faith madam, they left me just so to day, all alone by myself.

Enter O'Connor (*His arm bound*) *and Mrs.* Clermont

Oh, your most obedient, ladies and gentlemen. We shouldn't have found your snug airy drawing room here, only for that pretty little lustre that hangs up there. (*Sees Rangely.*) Ah! is that yourself? Faith! you fight like a lion, and run like an antelope. Is it so? You've got her; well, give me your hand, you've won her. Fight with an Irishman, and he's your friend for ever. Och, good luck to you! you've found the way to my heart through the hole you bored in my arm.

Mrs. C. I have yet had no opportunity of speaking to Mr. Campdon. This suspense is dreadful. [*To widow.*

Wid. Fr. Be content: this moment will end it.

Mrs. C. How?

Wid. Fr. Dear madam, collect your spirits. Your husband—

Enter Sydney *with* Osbert

Mrs. Clermont gazes intently on Osbert.

Syd. (*Presenting.*) My father.

Clar. Father! [*Runs to his arms.*

Camp. My friend Osbert!

Mrs. C. Merciful Heaven!

[*Almost overcome by her emotion.*

Osb. Yes, the poor Osbert.

Mrs. C. Osbert! [*Attempting to approach him.*

Osb. Ha! whose voice? Once again let me hear that voice.

Mrs. C. Osbert—oh! lead me—husband!

Osb. Great God! my Adelaide! my wife! make way there. Children, your mother!

[*Rushes to her with Sydney and Clara. She falls on his neck. Sydney and Clara kneel at her side. The curtain falls.*]

THE END

X
SUMMARY

As a literary figure, Barker's position is primarily determined by his work as a playwright. While he is more frequently referred to as a poet, critic and prose writer during his own times, his favorite literary medium was the drama, and into it he has put his most enthusiastic and successful efforts. It is there that his style acquires a deft competence of unmistakable finish. The plays best illustrate his originality of material, his independence and forcefulness. Their high seriousness, patriotism and swift precision in some cases, with their crisp wit and happy charm in others, are the most adequate embodiment of his literary personality.

It is in the field of dramatic literature that he has wielded the most extended and lasting influence. His leadership in the development of the native plays was a powerful determinant in the nature of American drama before the Civil War. His early treatment of Indian, Colonial and social material is reflected, directly or indirectly, in many later dramatists who exploited those themes. Custis, Bird, Stone, Mathews, and R. P. Smith are instances. Aside from any other considerations, Barker's historical importance and interest in the growth of American drama give him a high position among the early native dramatists. He mainly established this position between the years 1804 and 1824. From *Tears and Smiles*, the earliest of the plays to come down to us, through *The Indian Princess*, *Marmion*, and *The Court of Love*, to *Superstition* there is a steady, sure accumulation of power that places *Superstition* above any American play before 1825.

While Barker's non-dramatic poetry deserves a better lot than has been its fate of neglect, it has less of the historical significance of the dramas. A proportion of it is in the general trend of much of the verse composed in that day for albums and annuals and built around reproductions of engravings to be used as illustrations in New Year gift books. It contains, frequently, facile phrasing, graceful movement and quite charming moods but fails of greatness. The occasional odes and songs are more distinctive, but have lost in vitality as the events that inspired them have faded into the past. Their relative merits, however, as judged by the standards of other similar verse of the era, are high. The majority of the poems were composed during the years 1827 to 1836.

The prose writing is chronologically the most extensive. The first serious work appeared in 1816 while after 1837 there is little, at least that has survived, other than personal letters. There is a noticeable variety in tone and material. The biographical and historical pieces are more sober and carefully wrought. Their style is elaborated and less spontaneous than in other prose forms. The dramatic criticism is spirited and decisive, and, in instances of controversy, suavely stinging and aggressive. It was created in part as current comment upon plays appearing on the Philadelphia stage. It possesses the clarity of new made impressions tinged by a belief in well established dramatic principles. The flare of the theatre crowd is in it now and then. The orations, as customary, at the time, are fiery with militant patriotism and decorated with far-flung oratorical flights. Cannon salutes and the cheers of Democrats echo there. The political prose is tense with partisan feeling but usually well rooted in logical reasoning and historical knowledge. At times of political campaigning it is, however, slashing in its direct methods of attack; and in some cases, even in that era of unrestrained political attacks and counter-attacks, was "vetoed as too strong." There is, though, little bitter individual animosity. The personal correspondence is the most appealing of the prose. The less formal, more intimate letter form emphasizes the generosity, affection and high honor that were at the basis of Barker's character.

The principles of social and political democracy, of altruism and independence are unifying elements running through everything that Barker wrote. His aggressiveness, even belligerency; his conscientious honesty and unchanging ideals are part of his literary individuality. But foremost in his point of view is a sturdy, unswerving patriotism. First and last he believes in America. Her people, institution and traditions are just as worthy, in his eyes, of a place in literature as those of any other age or nation.

XI
BIBLIOGRAPHY

I. *CHRONOLOGICAL LISTS OF THE WORKS OF J. N. BARKER*

1. *Plays*

The Spanish Rover, one act completed, neither printed nor played, burned, 1804.

America, a one act masque, neither printed nor played, lost, 1805.

Attila, two acts, unfinished, neither printed nor played, lost, 1805.

Tears and Smiles, first acted March 4, 1807, printed New York and Philadelphia, 1808.

The Embargo; or, What News?, first acted March 16, 1808, not printed, lost, 1808.

The Indian Princess; or, La Belle Sauvage, first acted April 6, 1808, printed Philadelphia, 1808; reprinted in Moses, M. J., *Representative Plays by American Dramatists,* I, 573–628, New York, 1918.

Travellers; or, Music's Fascination, adapted or Americanized from Cherry, first acted December 26, 1808, not printed, lost, 1808.

Marmion; or, The Battle of Flodden Field, first acted April 13, 1812, printed New York, 1816; and Philadelphia, 1826.

The Armourer's Escape; or, Three Years at Nootka Sound, first acted March 21, 1817, not printed, lost, 1817.

How to Try a Lover, first acted March 26, 1836 under the title *A Court of Love,* printed New York, 1817.

Superstition; or, The Fanatic Father, first acted March 12, 1824, printed Philadelphia 1826; reprinted in Quinn, A. H., *Representative American Plays,* pp. 109–140, New York, 1917.

2. *Poems*

Columbia—Land of Liberty, song, printed in *Aurora,* Philadelphia, July 4, 1808.

SONG ("Ye patriots of Columbia"), *Democratic Press*, Philadelphia, July 7, 1809.

THE EXILE'S WELCOME, *Democratic Press*, Philadelphia, July 10, 1816.

THE DAY—*Ibid.*

ODE TO LAFAYETTE, broadside, printed from a wagon press during a parade in Philadelphia, September 28, 1824; reprinted in *National Gazette*, Philadelphia, September 30, 1824.

THE PILGRIMS OF PENNSYLVANIA, *Democratic Press*, Philadelphia, October 31, 1825.

PROLOGUE to James McHenry's *The Usurper*, printed in *The Casket*, Philadelphia, February, 1828; reprinted with the play, Philadelphia, 1829.

LITTLE RED RIDING HOOD, *Atlantic Souvenir*, pp. 97–101, Philadelphia, 1828; reprinted in Keese, *Poets of America*, New York, 1841.

PROLOGUE to R. P. Smith's *The Eighth of January*, Philadelphia, 1829.

THE BATTLE OF NEW ORLEANS, *American Sentinel*, Philadelphia, January 14, 1829.

LOVE ASLEEP, *Atlantic Souvenir*, pp. 16–22, Philadelphia, 1829; reprinted in *The Philadelphia Book*, 1836.

THE POWER OF LOVE, *Atlantic Souvenir*, p. 119, Philadelphia, 1829; partially reprinted, *Lady's Amaranth*, II, 32, Philadelphia, 1839.

HESITATION, a song, *Atlantic Souvenir*, p. 207, Philadelphia, 1829.

THE THREE SISTERS, *Atlantic Souvenir*, p. 130, Philadelphia, 1830 (appeared September, 1829); reprinted *American Sentinel*, Philadelphia, September 23, 1829.

THE GIPSEYING PARTY, *Atlantic Souvenir*, p. 87, Philadelphia, 1830; reprinted in *Godey's Lady's Book*, Philadelphia, February 1832; *American Sentinel*, Philadelphia, February 29, 1832.

ARCADIA, *Atlantic Souvenir*, pp. 210–216, Philadelphia, 1831.

LAS MUSICAS, *Atlantic Souvenir*, p. 324, Philadelphia, 1831.

THE MINSTREL, *Atlantic Souvenir*, pp. 194–196, Philadelphia, 1831.

LORD BYRON IN EARLY YOUTH, *Atlantic Souvenir,* p. 140, Philadelphia, 1832.

ODE, TO AN OLD HICKORY, *Hazard's Register of Pennsylvania,* Vol. 6, p. 330, Philadelphia, November 20, 1830.

ODE, THE BIRTH DAY OF WASHINGTON, printed from a wagon press printed in *American Sentinel,* Philadelphia, February 24, 1832.

ODE, FOR THE CENTENNIAL CELEBRATION OF THE FOUNDATION OF THE STATE IN SCHUYLKILL, May 1, 1832, printed in *Poulson's American Daily Advertiser,* Philadelphia, May 5, 1832; reprinted in *A History of the Schuylkill Fishing Company,* Philadelphia, 1889.

ADDRESS OF THE CARRIERS OF THE PENNSYLVANIAN, broadside, printed January 1, 1836; reprinted in *Daily Pennsylvanian,* Philadelphia, January 2, 1836.

ODE TO FRANCE, printed during a parade in Washington, April 24, 1848; reprinted in *Daily Union,* Washington, April 25, 1848.

ODE FOR THE COMMEMORATION OF THE LANDING OF PENN, broadside, n.d., Keys Collection, Baltimore.

3. *Prose*

THE DRAMA, eleven critical articles, *Democratic Press,* Philadelphia, December 18, 1816 to February 19, 1817.

DELAPLAINE'S REPOSITORY OF THE LIVES AND PORTRAITS OF DISTINGUISHED AMERICAN CHARACTERS, Vol. I, Part II, Philadelphia, 1817. (Six biographies—Peyton Randolph, Thomas Jefferson, John Jay, Rufus King, DeWitt Clinton, Robert Fulton) DeWitt Clinton, reprinted in *The Casket,* Philadelphia, September, 1827; Robert Fulton, *ibid.,* May, 1827; Rufus King, *ibid.,* July, 1827; John Jay, *ibid.,* August, 1829; Peyton Randolph, *ibid.,* July, 1830.

ORATION, July 4, 1817, printed *Democratic Press,* Philadelphia, July 8, 1817, pamphlet, Philadelphia, 1817.

ORATION, Philadelphia, July 4, 1824.

ORATION, Philadelphia, July 4, 1827.

SKETCHES OF THE PRIMITIVE SETTLEMENTS ON THE RIVER DELA-

WARE, Philadelphia, 1827; reprinted in *Hazard's Register of Pennsylvania,* Vol. I, p. 179, Philadelphia, 1828.

Series of political articles, *American Sentinel,* Philadelphia, May 21, 24, 30, 1831.

To WILLIAM DUNLAP, ESQ., June 10, 1832, Philadelphia, printed in William Dunlap, *History of the American Theatre,* pp. 376–380, New York, 1832. This is an account of Barker's own dramatic work.

Political article, *Daily Pennsylvanian,* Philadelphia, July 10, 1832.

To THE DEMOCRATIC CITIZENS OF PENNSYLVANIA, a series of five open letters. Four printed in *Daily Pennsylvanian,* Philadelphia, March 22, April 5, April 12, May 3, 1834. A fifth in ms June, 1834, Keys Collection, Baltimore.

ORATION, January 8, 1835, printed *Daily Pennsylvanian,* Philadelphia, January 16, 1835.

II. *SOURCE MATERIALS FOR THE BARKER PLAYS*

ARMOURER'S ESCAPE; OR, THREE YEARS AT NOOTKA SOUND, THE

Jewitt, John R., *A Narrative of the Adventures of John R. Jewitt during a Captivity of Three Years among the Savages of Nootka Sound with an Account of the Natives,* New York, 1816.

EMBARGO, OR WHAT NEWS, THE

Murphy, Arthur, *The Upholsterer,* in *Modern British Drama,* Vol. V, London, 1811.

HOW TO TRY A LOVER

Pigault-Lebrun, Guillaume Charles Antoine, *La Folie Espagnole,* 4 vols., Paris, 1812–1814.

INDIAN PRINCESS; OR, LA BELLE SAUVAGE, THE

Smith, Captain John, *The General History of Virginia,* London, 1624.

MARMION; OR, THE BATTLE OF FLODDEN FIELD

Holinshed, Raphael, *Chronicles of England, Scotland, and Ireland,* Vol. V, pp. 460–483.

Lindesay, Robert, *History of Scotland,* Reign of James IV, pp. 145–184, Edinburgh, 1778.

Scott, Sir Walter, *The Poetical Works,* Vol. II, Boston, 1871.

SUPERSTITION; OR, THE FANATIC FATHER

Burr, George Lincoln, ed., *Narratives of the Witchcraft Cases, 1648–1706* (Original Narratives of Early American History, Vol. XV), New York, 1917.

Calef, Robert, *More Wonders of the Invisible World,* Salem, 1823.

Collections of the Massachusetts Historical Society, Fourth Series, Vol. VIII.

Hutchinson, Thomas, *The History of Massachusetts,* 2 vols., Boston, 1795.

Mudge, Z. A., *Witch Hill,* New York, 1870.

National Cyclopaedia of American Biography, Vol. XI, New York, 1909.

Nevins, Winfield S., *Witchcraft in Salem Village 1692,* Salem, 1892.

Proceedings of the Massachusetts Historical Society, 1791–1855, Vol. 1.

Woodward, W. E., *Records of Salem Witchcraft Copied from the Original Documents,* 2 Vols., Roxbury, Mass., 1864–1865.

TEARS AND SMILES

Tyler, Royall, *The Contrast,* reprinted in Quinn, A. H., *Representative American Plays,* New York, 1917.

THE TRAVELLERS; OR, MUSIC'S FASCINATION

Cherry, A., *The Travellers; or, Music's Fascination* in *The New English Drama,* Vol. XXVII, London, 1823.

III. *BIOGRAPHY AND CRITICISM*

Anon. *Biographical Sketch*—a combined account of General John Barker and Major J. N. Baker, typewritten, n.d. [1858], Keys Collection, Baltimore.

Appleton's Cyclopaedia of American Biography, Vol. I, 165, New York, 1887.

Biggs, James, *History of Don Francesco de Miranda's Attempt to Effect a Revolution in South America,* Boston, 1810.

Encyclopedia Americana, Vol. II, Chicago and New York, 1903.

Evening Bulletin, Philadelphia, July 23, 1907.

Gentleman's Magazine, The, Vol. XL, 561, London, 1820.

Griscom, Rachel D., " John Barker," a biographical sketch printed in *The North American and the United States Gazette,* Philadelphia, January 14, 1876.

Heitman, F. B., *Historical Register and Dictionary of the United States Army,* Vol. I, 190, Washington, Government Printing Office, 1903.

London Review, The, pp. 78, 544, London, 1820.

Mease, James, *A Reply to the Criticism by J. N. Barker on the Historical Facts in the Picture of Philadelphia,* Philadelphia, 1828.

Moses, M. J., *The American Dramatist,* pp. 61, 74, 87, 135, Boston, 1925.

Moses, M. J., *Representative Plays by American Dramatists,* Vol. I, pp. 567–571, New York, 1918.

National Cyclopaedia of American Biography, Vol. XII, 276, New York, 1904.

Pennsylvania Magazine of History and Biography, Vol. XVII (1893), pp. 131–143; Vol. XLIV, Philadelphia (1925), 91–92.

Quinn, A. H., *A History of the American Drama from the Beginning to the Civil War,* pp. 136–151, 406 (containing a bibliography), New York, 1923.

Quinn, A. H., *Representative American Plays,* pp. 111–112, New York, 1917.

Reese, James, *Dramatic Authors of America, The,* pp. 21–24, Philadelphia, 1845.

Rogers, J. S., *James Rogers of New London Ct. and Descendants,* 234, Boston, 1902.

Shourds, Thomas, " John Barker," biographical comment printed in *The North American and the United States Gazette,* Philadelphia, January 14, 1876.

Simpson, Henry, *Lives of Eminent Philadelphians Now Deceased,* pp. 25–29, Philadelphia, 1859.

Theatrical Censor and Critical Miscellany, pp. 65, 81, Philadelphia, 1806.

Wescott, Thompson, " John Barker," biographical comments printed in *The North American and the United States Gazette*, Philadelphia, Jan. 14, 1876.

IV. *CORRESPONDENCE*

Barker, J. N., Ten ms letters, 1806–1830, Historical Society of Pennsylvania.

Barker, J. N., ms letter, January 31, 1820, Ridgway Library.

Barker, J. N., Twenty ms letters, 1807–1851, to General John Barker and Mrs. R. B. Keys, his daughter, Keys Collection, Baltimore.

Barker, Mrs. J. N., ms letter to Mrs. Rachel Jackson, 1837, Keys Collection, Baltimore.

Barker, John, Thirteen ms letters, 1806–1813, Historical Society of Pennsylvania.

Miscellaneous. Thirty-three ms letters, 1807–1858, to Barker, J. N.; Barker, Mrs. J. N.; Keys, Mrs. R. B. by Binns, John; Blake, Geo. E.; Blissett, W.; Brodhead, J. W.; Buchanan, James; Cadwalader, Thom.; Carr, Benj.; Clarke, J. C.; Cooper, T. A.; Dallas, G. M.; Delaplaine, J.; Duane, W. J.; Godey, L. A.; Jackson, Mrs. Rachel; Jenkins, Hannah C.; Kane, J. K.; Lawson, James; Littell, W.; McClellan, G.; Mease, James; Neagle, John; North, Miss; Randall, A.; Richards, Benj.; Vogdes, Jacob; Warren, W.; Watson, J. F.; Wood, W. B.; in the ms collections at the Historical Society of Pennsylvania, at the home of Keys, Miss Josephine, Baltimore; in the University of Pennsylvania Library; and the Ridgway Branch of the Philadelphia Library Company.

Philadelphia Custom House *Letter Books*. These are bound volumes of letters in the archives of the Custodian of Records.

1. *Correspondence, The Departments with the Collector,* ms, 17 bound vols., 1829–1844.
2. *Correspondence with the Secretary of the Treasury—Entry of Goods,* ms, 2 bound vols., 1835–1837.
3. *Seizure Suits,* ms, 1 bound vol., 1839.
4. *Correspondence—General,* ms, 1 bound vol., 1832.
5. *Marine Hospital,* ms, 1 bound vol., 1802–1837.

6. *Correspondence Rail Road Iron-Collector's Office,* ms, 8 bound vols., 1829–1843.
7. *Circular Letters from the Treasury Department,* printed forms, 4 vols., 1829, 1837, 1838–41, 1842–43.
8. *Seizure Suits at Law, Collector's Office,* ms, 2 bound vols., 1830–1831.
9. *Correspondence—Fines, Forfeitures, and Penalties,* ms, 1 bound vol., 1833 (3d quarter).

V. *HISTORIES AND ARCHIVES*

1. *General Accounts and Records*

Beard, Chas. A. and Mary R., *Rise of American Civilization, The,* 2 vols., New York, 1927.

Biennial Register of All Officers and Agents, Civil, Military, and Naval in the Service of the United States, prepared at the Department of State, 12 vols., 1837–1859, Washington, D. C.

Journals and Documents of the United States Senate and House of Representatives.

Executive Documents, 27th Congress, 3d Session, Vol. 5, 1842–1843, Washington, D. C.

Journal of the Executive Proceedings of the Senate, Vol. II, 1805–1815, Washington, 1828.

Journal of the Senate, Vol. IV, 1805–1811, Washington, 1821.

Journal of the Executive Proceedings of the Senate of the United States of America, Vols. V–VI, 1837–1845, Washington, 1887.

Journal of the House of Representatives, Vol. VII, 1809–1811, Washington, 1826.

Journal of the House of Representatives, 27th Congress, Second Series, p. 1428, August 26, 1843.

Mayo, R., *United States Fiscal Department,* 2 vols., Washington, 1847.

McCulloh, R. P., *Military Operations on the Delaware,* pp. 4–5, Philadelphia, 1820.

Treasury Department

Files—Office of the Secretary—Division of Appointments, Washington, D. C., Barker, James N.

Secretaries of the Treasury, Assistant Secretaries of the Treasury and Presidents under Whom They Served, pamphlet, No. 70073, issued by the Treasury Department, 1921.

War Department

Records, Adjutant General's Office, War Department, Washington, D. C., Barker, James N.

Files, Adjutant General's Office, War Department, Washington, D. C., Barker, James N.

2. *Pennsylvania and Philadelphia*

Buchanan Papers

Collection of the Historical Society of Pennsylvania, manuscript section.

By Laws, Muster Roll and Papers Selected from the Archives of First Troop, Philadelphia Cavalry, pp. 39, 40, 42, Philadelphia, 1856.

Charter and By Laws of the Historical Society of Pennsylvania, contains all officers and members, Philadelphia, 1880.

Genealogical Society of Pennsylvania Collections.

Burial Records, Board of Health, Philadelphia, 1815–1824.

Christ Church Records, Philadelphia, Vol. VI, burials, 1785–1900.

Notices of Marriages and Deaths in Poulson's American Daily and General Advertiser, 5 vols., 1791–1833.

Lewis, J. F., *History of the Apprentice's Library of Philadelphia,* p. 10, Philadelphia, 1924.

Memoirs of the Historical Society of Pennsylvania, Vol. I, Part I, 11, Philadelphia, 1826.

Minutes of the Secretary of the Committee of Defence, 1814, ms, Historical Society of Pennsylvania.

History of the Schuylkill Fishing Company, Philadelphia, 1889.

Laurel Hill Cemetery Company's Records—Vital statistics for J. N. Barker and all of his immediate family, 1837–1858.

Oberholtzer, E. P., *Philadelphia, A History of the City and Its People,* 4 vols., Philadelphia, n.d.

Oberholtzer, E. P., *Literary History of Philadelphia,* Philadelphia, 1906.

Olympic Theatre, Proceedings and Resolutions, Philadelphia, 1819.

Papers of the Mayors of Philadelphia.

Manuscript Collection Historical Society of Pennsylvania. 17 items—letters, petitions and receipts of John Barker, 1805–1813; 3 letters to the City Councils, J. N. Barker, 1820.

Pennsylvania Archives.

Pennsylvania Archives, Second Series, IX, 338.

Pennsylvania Archives, Sixth Series, I, 111, 239, 474; III, 947; IV, 64, 758, 770; V, 495.

Philadelphia Municipal Records.

Archives of the Recorder of Deeds and of the Register of Wills, City Hall, Philadelphia.

Play Bills.

Collection of the Historical Society of Pennsylvania, 1820–1839, Philadelphia theatres.

Sharf and Wescott, *History of Philadelphia,* 3 vols., Philadelphia, 1884. (Exhaustive index, Vol. III.)

Watson, J. F., *Annals of Philadelphia and Pennsylvania in the Olden Times,* 2 vols., Philadelphia, 1884.

Wescott, Thompson, *Civil Officers of Philadelphia and Pennsylvania,* Vol. I, 51, 264, 266; Vol. II, 5, 75, ms, Historical Society of Pennsylvania.

Westcott, Thompson, *History of Free Masonry in Philadelphia,* p. 27 (clippings), Historical Society of Pennsylvania.

Wescott, Thompson, *Historical Scrap Book* (newspaper clippings) Vol. I, 87, Historical Society of Pennsylvania.

Young, J. R., *Memorial History of the City of Philadelphia,* I, 432, 443, 420; II, 162, New York, 1895.

3. *Histories of the Theatre*

Alterations and Amendments in the Articles and Plan of the Association of Proprietors of the Olympic Theatre, Philadelphia, 1821.

Diary or Daily Account Book of W. B. Wood, 1810–1835, incomplete, 9 vols., ms, University of Pennsylvania Library.

Dunlap, William, *History of the American Theatre,* pp. 308–316, New York, 1832.

Durang, Charles, *The Philadelphia Stage From the Year 1749 to the Year 1855,* published in three series in the *Sunday Dispatch,* Philadelphia, 1854, 1856, 1860. First series includes the history for 1749–1821, the second 1822–1830, the third 1830–1855. It is not published in book form but complete files are pasted in six volumes in the University of Pennsylvania Library.

Genest, John, *Some Account of the English Stage, 1660–1830,* Vol. IX, 83–84, London, 1832.

Hornblow, Arthur, *A History of the Theatre in America from its Beginnings to the Present Time,* II, 55, 58, Philadelphia, 1919.

Ireland, J. N., *Records of the New York Stage from 1750 to 1860,* Vol. I, 258–259, 283; II, 455, New York, 1866.

Modern British Drama, V, 439–452 (Murphy, *The Upholsterer*), London, 1811.

Odell, J. C. D., *Annals of the New York Stage,* 4 vols., New York, 1927.

Wegelin, Oscar, *Early American Plays,* Dunlap Society Publications, series 2, X, 10–12, New York, 1900.

Wemyss, F. C., *Twenty-six Years of the Life of an Actor and Manager,* 2 vols., New York, 1847.

Wood, W. B., *Personal Recollections of the Stage,* Philadelphia, 1855.

VI. *NEWSPAPER FILES*

1. *Baltimore*

Sun, The, 1848, 1858.

2. *London*

Times, The, 1820–1821.

3. *Philadelphia*

American Sentinel, 1828–1829, 1831–1832.

Aurora, 1800, 1806–1808, 1812–1814, 1816–1817, 1820.

Chronicle, Daily, 1830.
Democratic Press, 1807–1811, 1813–1829.
Evening Bulletin, 1858, 1907, 1927.
Evening Journal, 1858.
Franklin Gazette, 1818.
Freeman's Journal, 1808.
National Gazette and Literary Register, 1824, 1828, 1830–1831.
North American and United States Gazette, 1858, 1876.
Pennsylvania Inquirer, 1858.
Pennsylvania Inquirer and Morning Journal, 1830.
Pennsylvanian, Daily, 1832–1839, 1841–1842, 1848, 1858.
Philadelphia Gazette, 1830.
Philadelphia Press, 1858.
Poulson's Daily Advertiser, 1808, 1819, 1830, 1837–1838.
Public Ledger, 1837, 1842, 1858.
Sunday Dispatch, 1808, 1858.
Tickler, The, 1808.
True American, 1806.
United States Gazette, 1808–1810, 1828–1829, 1836, 1838.

4. *Washington*, *D. C.*

Congressional Globe, 1842.
Globe, Daily, 1838, 1840–1845, 1857–1858.
National Advertiser, Daily, 1858.
National Intelligencer, Daily, 1841–1842, 1848–1849, 1858.
Union, Daily, 1845–1857.

VII. *PERIODICALS*

1. *London*

Annual Register or a View of the History, Politics and Literature of the Year 1820, London, 1820.
European Magazine and London Review, Vol. 78, 1820.
Gentleman's Magazine, Vol. XL, 1820.
New Monthly Magazine and Literary Journal, Vol. III, 1821.

2. *Philadelphia*

Album and Ladies Weekly Gazette, Vols. I–VIII, 1826–1834.
American Quarterly Review, Vol. 1, 1827.
Analectic Magazine, Vols. I–XIII, 1813–1818.
Godey's Lady's Book, Vol. IV, 1832.
Hazard's Register of Pennsylvania, Vol. I, 1838; Vol. VI, 1830; Vol. XIII, 1834.
Ladies Literary Port Folio, Vol. I, Nos. 1–2, December, 1828.
Pennsylvania Magazine of History and Biography, Vol. IV, 1880; Vol. XVII, 1893; Vol. XXVI, 1902; Vol. XLVI, 1922; Vol. XLIX, 1925.
Port Folio, Vols. IX–XXII, 1820–1828.
Saturday Evening Post, February 1, 1823–January 31, 1824.
Theatrical Censor and Critical Miscellany, Philadelphia, 1806.
Trangram or Fashionable Trifler, Vol. I, Nos. 1–2, 1809.

INDEX

INDEX

INDEX